A natural storyteller, Mark takes you on a journey through his own experiences as a CEO of realizing that relationships are more important than transactions, and the workplace should be a place you want to go versus a place you have to be.

KEITH FERRAZZI
Global thought leader
Speaker and author

Mark Chamberlain, "A Man For All Seasons," has finally put into written word what for him has been an incredible ride from misunderstood youth to industry leader and people leader.

If you ever wanted to see, in action, the results of what goes around comes around, learn from Mark how in adding to other's experiences, you add to your own.

The good news is if you read this book, you might learn how to be successful at financial planning, but for sure you'll learn how to be successful at life.

WILL GLAROS
Founding partner, Meyers Glaros Group
WJOB radio host
Guest columnist, Hammond Times

Why Do I Work Here? *will show you that you have to bring the right talent into your organization, and more importantly, gain their loyalty and engagement over time. Mark's experiences will enrich your perspectives about talent management and how purpose is the glue that makes everything come together.*

TIM SANDERS

New York Times *bestselling author,* Love is the Killer App: How to Win Business and Influence Friends

In Why Do I Work Here?, *Mark has laid out a compelling argument that getting the most from your business requires you to make the most of your culture. Forget carrots and sticks, the future belongs to those who create a culture that promotes autonomy, free thinking, and collaboration.*

DENNIS MOSELEY-WILLIAMS

Principal, DWM Strategic Consulting

WHY DO I
WORK
HERE?

WHY DO I
WORK
HERE?

Transformative Thought About
BUSINESS CULTURE and **RELATIONSHIPS**

Lance — Patti & Jacob thought
you might enjoy this read —
please share your thoughts
after you read it!
Best,

MARK W. CHAMBERLAIN

Printed in the United States of America.
Library of Congress Control Number: 2020905038
ISBN: 978-1-73448-865-4

Layout by David Taylor.
Cover by Wesley Strickland.

I would like to humbly thank my family, friends, coworkers, and literally hundreds of other authors, speakers, and generally inspirational people who made this book possible.
Also, thanks Mom and Dad ... and Lou!

Contents

You Have to Know You Have a Problem before You Can Look for a Solution

I am the CEO of Lakeside Wealth Management in Chesterton, Indiana, a small town near Chicago. We enjoy the proximity of the big city and the comfort of small town living as well as a rich pool of talent to employ. As Lakeside grew, we learned a lot about human capital in terms of hiring, training, engaging, and retaining people. It has been quite an education so far, but we know there is much more to learn.

As it turns out, much of what we have learned so far applies not just to our people but to almost everyone else as well—clients, family, friends, and even strangers.

It mostly comes down to one fact: people desire to be connected.

What I will share in the following pages is our journey to create a more dynamic workplace and more meaningful engagement. If the process is addressed diligently and constantly, the end result is a better experience not only for your employees and coworkers but for your customers, family, and friends. I will share with you the strategies and philosophies that have worked—and some that have not.

The most important characteristic of a business is the willingness to acknowledge that getting better is your only real option for survival. Realize that if *better* exists, *best* never can.

Dozens of authors and speakers have contributed to our journey in some way—many mentioned specifically in this book. This is an important point not just for gratitude but because as humans, we become what we learn. We become an amalgam of *all* our experiences and, in turn, allow those whom we touch to add exponentially to their experiences. This is an unstoppable and ageless fact. For every person we touch or interact with, there is an imprint of us on their lives as well as their imprint on ours. Whether that imprint is good or bad is more in our control than we realize.

I am sure that some readers' reactions to some of these interpersonal concepts will range from "brilliant" to "crazy," and I will appreciate and learn from both.

Finally, please consider the following pages with an open, flexible, and fearless mind. My hope is that by enriching your relationships, you may simultaneously change your business and your life.

PART ONE

Evolution of the Mindset

CHAPTER 1

Up Battle Creek
without a Paddle

We don't realize our lives as they happen; we cobble
them together after a series of years, experiences,
successes, failures, and—always—questions.

—MARK W. CHAMBERLAIN

We're all born into circumstances we can't control, and those circumstances shape who we are and how we approach life.

I was born in Saint Joseph, Michigan, and my family moved to Battle Creek when I was two. From age two until I was four or five, we lived in a government housing project in Battle Creek, Michigan. Between our eight-plex apartment building and the one next to it, there was a dirt lot—no grass or anything—where the kids played. Every time you went outside, you'd get filthy—but we were happy.

In their own ways, both my parents shaped me into who I am today—through both positive and negative influences. Sometimes my mom would call me inside, give me a dollar, and say, "Hey, go to the store and buy me some cigarettes." In those days, a pack of cigarettes was thirty cents. So I'd have enough money to buy three packs of cigarettes and a candy bar for five cents and still get a nickel back from the dollar. I'd make the long trek down the lot, across a set of railroad tracks, through a field, and through the parking lot of a mall to the convenience store. It probably wasn't that far, but on the legs of a four-year-old, it was a journey. And I'd return with the cigarettes for my mom, a candy bar, and a nickel in my pocket.

My dad was a traveling salesman and was gone a lot, and Mom worked two jobs just to keep us three kids (and a fourth on the way) fed. Because my dad was always away and Mom had to work so much, any time we weren't in school, us older kids would be shipped off to our grandparents—me to my paternal grandmother and my sister to my maternal grandmother, while Mom kept the baby with her. We'd be away a week here and a week there while school was in session, and after school let out, we'd be sent away for most of the summer.

My grandmother had a picture of me as a small child, holding her hand and crying. I remember standing there thinking, "Why doesn't Mom want me? Why does she always take me here? Why doesn't Mom love me?"

Now I loved my grandma, and she was great to me, but in my four-year-old mind, the fact that my mother was always sending me away made me feel unloved and unlovable. In the present (adulthood), that would be a rather silly and rash conclusion to draw, but that was my perception as a child, and as a result, it was one of the early decisions I came to about myself.

Because of this, I did not have a great relationship with my mom over the years. She was not really emotionally available, for her own reasons; I think I saw her cry only once or twice in her life. We were functional, but we were not really close.

My mom passed away in 2013. About six months before she got sick, my therapist and a dear friend convinced me to go down to visit her in Indianapolis, where she was living then. For the three months before I went, I worked on a carefully crafted sentence that would communicate exactly what I wanted to say to her. I had my memory of being a four-year-old in 1964 but had never asked her for her memory of that time.

I traveled to Indianapolis and took my mom out to lunch. As we ate, I said to her, "I want to ask you one question."

"Oh God," she said. "What's the matter? What did I do?"

"Nothing," I said. "Relax. It's just one question: What was going on in your life in 1964?"

I didn't ask, "Why did you do this; why did you do that?" I didn't ask, "Why did you leave me all the time when I was four?" I didn't say, "You made me feel unloved and unlovable."

I just asked, "What was going on in your life in 1964?"

"Oh," said my mom, sitting back. "1964 ..." Her eyes darted through the air as her mind started moving down memory lane. And then she started talking—*for an hour and a half!* She spilled out all the things that had been going on in her life when I was a little kid. Personal things, struggles with my dad, money problems—and more. Some of it I knew, but much of it was completely new to me.

We connected like we never had before, because I now understood what she was going through as a woman and not as the mommy of a four-year-old. And for the last six months of her life, things were really good between us. It was probably the best period in my life with my mom. And it became possible because I learned how to stop being invasive or accusatory—and by not allowing my four-year-old brain to be in charge. I managed to let my adult brain be in charge for a while. I just asked for clarity and listened.

This exercise helped me to understand what my mom was experiencing all those years ago when I was a little kid. It didn't change what I'd experienced—but now I had perspective. What I remember from when I was four years old is only what I saw through a four-year-old's eyes. Whatever happened to me, I drew conclusions in the moment and about the moment in my four-year-old mind.

It's quite difficult to change those conclusions now that I'm an adult, even with the perspective of my mom's side of the story. But it's from those experiences that I learned how to behave, that I learned how to misbehave, and that I learned how to survive.

Every time I succeed because of those learned behaviors, my childhood conclusions serve me well. Every time I fail because of those learned behaviors, my childhood conclusions limit me.

As a four-year-old kid, holding on to my grandmother's hand, my conclusion was that my mom didn't want me. And that created a big hole in me, a persistent feeling that no matter what I do, it's never enough, because *I* wasn't enough.

That feeling is something I had to learn to survive with—and it's shaped who I am. Because of that feeling, I've always been an overachiever. I've always pushed myself to do more, to be better, and that is part of how I got where I am today. But because of that feeling, I have also struggled with really finding my true value.

Knowing my mom's side of the story helped heal my relationship with her, but it didn't change that fundamental part of me.

* * *

Unfortunately, my dad passed away in 2011, and I never got to have the same conversation in the same way with him that I had with my mom—something I deeply regret. But my dad had an equally big influence on who I am today.

Growing up, we didn't have much. We didn't have toys, so I would figure out how to play with whatever my environment provided me. We didn't have money, so I just had to figure it out.

My dad encouraged this "figure it out" discipline when I was a teenager in the mid-1970s. Around that time we moved into a modest four-bedroom ranch house in Chesterton, Indiana, where we lived until I left for college. At the time, I thought we'd gone from poverty to upper middle class. It was only much later—almost forty years and only six months before my mother died—that I learned we had rented that house. In fact, we had always rented. My family never owned our own home. We never had the resources.

What I did know was that when I was a teenager, I usually didn't have the money to buy the things I wanted. In 1974, when I was fourteen years old, I'd earn what I could doing chores and odd jobs, making fifty cents per hour for babysitting my brothers and sisters—until I had amassed a fortune: twenty dollars!

When I was fourteen, almost all my buddies had bikes. And let me tell you, there was nothing I wanted more than to have a bike too. But we didn't have the money. We were doing better than when I was little, but we could still afford very little, and a bike certainly wasn't on the list.

One day I was bellyaching to my dad about wanting a bike. "Come on," I said. "I'm fourteen. Every one of my friends has a bike, and I don't." I had my twenty dollars saved, but a bike cost almost fifty dollars at the time. I was hoping I could convince my dad to match what I had saved. "I've got some money saved," I told my dad. "I just don't have enough."

My dad simply looked at me and said, "Make more money."

I was angry. I was insulted. I thought he was just being a smart-ass. Of course I needed to make more money!

It wasn't until much later that I realized he was being serious and that he was actually giving me some pretty deep advice—or at least, that's how I came to interpret it many years later. He was telling me that getting what I want is within my power. It was and will always be. It's up to me to make it happen, and I have control over that situation. I get to be in charge of what I have and what I don't have.

I didn't realize it at the time, but growing up in that environment made me a fighter. I was born into a situation where I had zero control, and I didn't run away or give up. Instead, I always chose to just fight and figure it out—because when I was a kid, there wasn't any other option.

And today, as a business owner, I still (try to) figure it out. I dropped out of college, so I was never trained to be a CEO of a financial services firm—or really anything else, to be honest. I learned it when I was forty; I figured it out. When the markets went really bad in 2001 and again in 2008, my wife said to me, "What if this goes off the tracks? What if it doesn't work out, and you've got to find something else?"

> One of the things my childhood taught me was that it doesn't matter what your circumstances are. You can have control over what happens—at least, more than you think.

"Listen," I said, "if I have to go flip burgers at McDonald's, I will, and in six months, I'll own the franchise. I don't know how, but I know I can figure it out." I know that power is in me because of my experiences growing up.

We can't control the circumstances we are born into. But one of the things my childhood taught me was that it doesn't matter what your circumstances are. You can have control over what happens—at least, more than you think.

As I became an adult, that lesson stayed with me. If I wanted something, it was up to me. I didn't have to depend on someone else. That sparked my entrepreneurial spirit and set me on the path to where I am today. And if I had not learned those lessons, many of the insights on the pages that follow would not have been possible.

Unfortunately, and fortunately, other lessons stayed with me also, and I soon found out that the learning was not over yet!

CHAPTER 2

The Early Training

When the student is ready, the teacher will appear.

—BUDDHIST PROVERB

Although I attended Wabash College in Crawfordsville, Indiana, on an academic scholarship, college was not where my real education happened.

The summer after my second year, I went looking for a summer job—with every intention of going back to school in the fall—but like most twenty-year-olds, I was easily distracted. I got on the train to Chicago, about an hour commute, looking for anything to take up my time and make some money for the summer. Almost entirely by accident, I ended up stumbling into the Chicago Board of Trade (CBOT). I actually walked into the building to grab some lunch at one of the restaurants in the lobby and saw that it had an observation deck where you could go and watch what was happening on the trading floor.

I didn't even really know what I was looking at, but man, it was exciting! Guys yelling and screaming, buying and selling, spitting and swearing—it was like the scene in *Trading Places*, but it was real!

"I don't even know what they're doing," I said to myself, "but that's what I want to do." (Did I mention I was easily distracted?)

I got into the elevator and rode up and down forty-some floors of the building until I finally convinced somebody to hire me as a clerk. They paid me a whopping $110 a week. I know it was 1980 dollars, but trust me—that was not a lot of money, even then. In fact, it was about half of what it cost me just to get to Chicago on the train every day—but it was worth it.

When fall rolled around, I was supposed to go back to school, but the broker I was working for said, "Listen, I'll double your salary if you stay for another semester." I said yes. Fall semester came to an end, and he said, "I'll double it again if you stay for another semester." I said yes again.

It was simultaneously both the dumbest and smartest thing I ever did.

In the end, I never went back to school. Instead, I stayed at the Chicago Board of Trade for the next nineteen years. I worked my way up to being a broker and a trader in the Treasury Bond Pit.

The pit at CBOT was a world unto itself. In fact, the "pit" is an accurately descriptive word for the trading floor. It was a mad, feral place, full of people yelling and pushing and swearing and spitting. When it was busy in the pit, the only rule was "me first." You were only as good as your last trade. It was a cutthroat environment in which you got rewarded for being ruthless. Getting the trade, no matter the cost, meant making money—and making money was the most important thing.

I don't want to vilify the CBOT—it helped make me what I

am—but it was a dog-eat-dog world. There was no long-lasting value to almost any of the relationships I formed there—as evidenced by the fact that I keep in touch with almost no one from those days. There were several hundred people in the pit with me for nearly twenty years. We knew each other's spouses and kids, but today, I keep in touch with only a handful.

What I learned was that a real relationship means actually caring about the other person. There's a difference between being "friends" with somebody and caring about them. Facebook friendships are the perfect example of this. Think about all the people you are "friends" with on Facebook. Do you really *care* about them? Do they really *care* about you?

You may know a lot about them—their kids' names, where they went on vacation last year, what they had for breakfast this morning—but just trading information about each other doesn't actually create a personal relationship. It's okay to have both types of relationships throughout your life—but just realize that there IS a difference.

There's a huge difference between knowing the facts about someone's life and really knowing them as a person. I stood in pretty much the same place with the same people for nineteen years at the CBOT. I stood

> There's a huge difference between knowing the facts about someone's life and really knowing them as a person.

next to these guys every day. We played golf together and went out to dinner sometimes. But we didn't really care about each other once the trading got tough again. All we cared about was where the next trade was coming from. There was little reward for investing time in a relationship.

I think this me-first culture was present in a lot of other workplaces at that time as well; the aggressiveness of the CBOT trading lifestyle just made it stand out more. What was out in the open at the CBOT, how people really felt, was often active beneath the surface in other office or workplace settings—something I discovered firsthand when I left CBOT.

In 1998, I retired from the Chicago Board of Trade at age thirty-eight. By that point, I was just burned out. I was successful at it, but it was a hard job, and it made life hard. The industry was also changing, so life on the floor was changing—the advancements in technology made being there in person obsolete for the most part. I had a few bucks saved—which was fortunate, because I had nowhere to go from there. I had learned a lot about money from being a bond trader, but I didn't have a degree, certification, or even experience to do anything else. I was thirty-eight with a wife, three kids, a house payment, and an extremely skimpy resume. Where was I going to find a job where I could make the kind of living I'd made being a trader?

I finally went to a friend who was a headhunter, and he did an assessment of my skills. The result? That I would be good at sales.

I almost wanted to vomit. I did not want to be a salesperson. (No offense meant to salespeople here, as I have discovered we are *all* in sales!)

"Well," said my friend, "let's figure out something that combines your personality with your financial background."

The result: I should become a financial advisor.

For about a year and a half, I didn't work. Instead, I studied, took my exams, and got the required licenses to be a financial advisor. In 2000, I joined a gentleman at a small local firm. He was older than me, and his intent was to sell me the firm when he retired.

Unfortunately, this guy was completely transaction oriented. We weren't in the pit anymore, but he came from the same me-first culture as me and my former colleagues. I was starting a new phase in my life, so I was in learning mode, and everything I learned from him reinforced my understanding that the world was transaction based. That was the only system I believed in; in fact, it was the only system I even knew existed.

In 2002, I decided to strike out on my own, and I started Lakeside Wealth Management. I didn't have any customers yet, but I had enough friends and connections that I was able to make things work. I was starting to get clients with higher net worth and more sophisticated financial needs. In 2004, I took on a new business partner, and things were looking good—but I was still operating from a place of me first.

I think a part of me always knew that there had to be a more meaningful type of work, a more meaningful type of workplace. But business was good, and it was hard to look beyond that. It was hard to even fathom that there was a whole other way of thinking about work, about life, and about the world. It never occurred to me that working on relationships and caring about my clients and coworkers in a deeper and more meaningful way would actually make work more enjoyable.

Then, in 2005, I read a book called *Never Eat Alone*, and nearly *everything* changed.

CHAPTER 3

My Never Eat Alone Moment

When I let go of what I am, I become what I might be.

—LAO TZE

Sometime in 2005, I went to a conference in Seattle. The keynote speaker was Keith Ferrazzi, who had just published his book *Never Eat Alone*, and everyone at the conference was given a copy. So on the plane ride back home to Chicago, I decided to crack open the book and do a little reading.

I read almost the entire book on that flight. I identified so strongly with most everything the author was writing about that I couldn't stop reading. Like me, he had grown up without much. He'd gotten his experience by caddying at a local country club, where he learned how to interact with people who had a lot more money than he did. And he soon realized that building a relationship was much more important than completing a transaction.

It's like the old proverb: if you give a man a fish, you feed him for a day; if you teach a man to fish, you feed him for a lifetime. A transaction is like giving a man a fish—it's a one-time interaction that gets a result at the moment but doesn't continue into the future. A relationship, on the other hand, can last a long time.

This change of attitude changed the course of Ferrazzi's life. He's had a very successful career as an executive, and now has his own consulting firm, Ferrazzi Greenlight, which focuses on the importance of relationships in business success—and he's published at least two best-selling books on the subject as well.

Reading *Never Eat Alone* was a revelation. I'd never even considered that I could approach work (and life!) from a standpoint that was relationship based rather than transaction based—that I could be relationship driven rather than transaction driven.

I developed a hunger to explore this topic by any means available. Over the next couple of years, I read everything I could get my hands on, from Ed Catmull's *Creativity, Inc.* to Simon Sinek's *Start With Why* to books by Daniel Pink and Malcolm Gladwell and Tim Sanders. (There are so many authors I am grateful to for inspiring this change that I've lost count!)

I watched TED Talks on the subject of relationship building. I went to conferences and absorbed everything I could. I was completely fascinated by the idea that life could be driven by interpersonal relationships rather than the need to sell things. This whole genre of leadership appealed to me, and I've since branched off into related topics such as coaching and team building. But the common thread has always been relationships.

Perhaps the biggest realization was that I needed to show up in the workplace with a similar approach. Many of us spend as much time with our coworkers as our families, so it occurred to me that was also a great place to start changing my behavior. Because of my leadership position, I realized that to some extent, my colleagues would be a reflection of me. What would that reflection look like?

After digesting numerous books, I gradually started trying to change how I behaved. My goal was to slow down a little bit. To be honest, I still struggle with this concept of slowing down and being in the moment. If I am like most people, the idea of going one hundred miles per hour because I'm always busy is not only bad for my health but bad for my relationships. Something had to change. But for this change to stick, I had to develop new habits and unlearn much of what the first twenty years of my career taught me.

It was tough at first, but I soon came to enjoy it. The more I treated people differently, it seemed, the more they wanted to be around me to some extent. (Duh!) The unavoidable conclusion was that I never realized how *unlikable* I was to be around before!

One of the earliest and biggest changes I made was my attitude when going to industry conferences. If you could have seen pictures of me at conferences before some of these changes, you'd notice that I'm always standing with my arms folded across my chest. This pose was a perfect illustration of my mindset, and although it was subliminal, my body language was sending a clear message to my peers. I wasn't willing to open up and share anything that was working for me, because I was operating from a mindset of scarcity. I thought that if I gave away what I had learned, then somehow, I wouldn't be able to outrun my competitors.

After reading Ferrazzi's book, I started to approach conferences in a different way. I would walk into a session not with my arms folded but with them outstretched. I was ready to talk to anybody, to hear what they had to say, and to share what I was doing in my own work.

One time, I sat with a fellow advisor, and we exchanged a couple of ideas about what I was doing with my company. Then I asked him, "What's your best idea?"

"I call all my clients and friends on their birthdays," he answered, "and I sing 'Happy Birthday' to them."

I had this conversation in late 2006, and since then, most everybody I know—clients, friends, colleagues, people I like—gets a call from me on their birthday. I make a point of finding out when people's birthdays are, and I put them into my calendar as recurring events. I probably make between one and five calls a day, usually while I'm on my way to work. It's a small but thoughtful gesture that doesn't cost me anything but time—and the response on the other end of the line is always amazing! Best of all, I got that idea from someone else who was willing to share because I had shared something with them first.

This small act is an example of the kinds of things that have been extremely helpful in developing, strengthening, and maintaining these relationships—and it's something I would never have considered as a good use of my time when I lived in a transaction-based, me-first mindset.

Now that I am more aware, I see that mindset at work in many places and situations. I still meet people who approach life with their arms crossed, afraid of giving anything away.

A year or so ago, I met a young man from a nearby town. He's a skilled advisor, and we seemed to share a common philosophy on how to approach our profession. I kept in touch with this advisor, and several months later, I sent him an invitation on LinkedIn. He didn't respond. A couple of weeks later I sent him another one—still no response. Finally, I called him and said, "Hey, I've been trying to connect with you on LinkedIn. Are you getting the notifications?"

"Oh yeah," he replied, "I got them. But I'd be crazy to connect with you. Then you'd have all my contacts!"

The fact of the matter is, I'm not going to gain anything by having access to his contacts, and he wouldn't lose anything by sharing with me. People do business with you because they like and trust you. But in the bigger picture, the advisor will lose more than just clients if he keeps that approach. It's just incredibly limiting.

This is the scarcity mindset in action. The scarcity mindset says that there's only so much pie to go around, so if you get more pie, it means that I will have less. The scarcity mindset says that if you are winning, I'm losing. It implies there's no such thing as a win-win situation.

That's just not true. My success doesn't automatically mean you're going to be unsuccessful. The fact that I'm doing well doesn't mean that you're automatically going to do poorly.

> The scarcity mindset says that if you are winning, I'm losing. It implies there's no such thing as a win-win situation.

A lot of scarcity thinking is related to money, but the mindset also extends to happiness (among other things), manifesting itself as a feeling that the happier you are, the less happiness there is for me. It seems ridiculous when you say it out loud, but subconsciously, it's what many people feel. And it is just not true. There's an unlimited amount of happiness in the world. And in fact, the more I have, the more I want to give away. Happiness is contagious.

It's not easy to shift out of a scarcity mindset, partly because of how we've been indoctrinated to measure success with things that are easy to measure—like money. What would happen if we took the focus off material things as a measurement of success? In Shakespeare's *Romeo and Juliet*, when the young lovers are declaring their love, Juliet says of her love, "My bounty is as boundless as the sea. The more I give to thee, the more I have, for both are infinite." The same is true of happiness. The scarcity mindset says, "The more I give, the less I have," but happiness functions from a place of abundance, and the abundance mindset says, "The more I give, the more I have."

As I started to shift my mindset away from transactions and me first and toward caring and building relationships—away from a scarcity mindset and toward a mindset of abundance—I found myself wanting to give more. One day I saw a picture of a member of my community giving a sizable check to a charity, and I felt a bolt of inspiration. I wanted to be able to do that—to give back to the community.

I'd lived here most of my life—even gone to high school here—but I had never really been a part of the community because although I *lived* in Chesterton, Indiana, I *worked* in Chicago. I'd go to work early in the morning and come home at night without really participating in neighborhood activities. I didn't volunteer, and I wasn't on any boards. I realized that I was taking advantage of all the good things my hometown had to offer but never giving anything back—not my time, talents, or treasures.

Once I started working closer to home, I began getting involved in the community around me. I started to interact with people who were involved in nonprofits. I started to care about the people around me and to develop meaningful relationships with them. Whatever charisma or energy I may have naturally possessed had been buried inside me. It wasn't until I was mentally open to this new way of thinking—when I opened my arms instead of keeping them crossed—that this energy came to life.

I soon found out that people wanted to be around that kind of energy. When you start building a reputation as someone who cares, people start coming to you for advice and mentorship. I found that people trusted me because I was willing to be vulnerable with them. In many cases, when someone is asking for advice, they are typically asking because they are in pain. Being vulnerable invites the other person to be vulnerable as well, which deepens the relationship and allows them to share their pain more comfortably. I had always known this in my personal life and felt like being vulnerable came naturally to me. But because of my early career, I just wasn't aware of how valuable vulnerability as a characteristic really can be in business until I started my journey in my second career. Now it's not just part of who I am but a tool I can use—a tool I'd had all along.

One thing Ferrazzi talks about in his book is paying it forward. Since 2005, when I was given *Never Eat Alone*, I am sure I have given away more than a thousand books, and I've recommended countless more when I didn't have a copy on hand to give to someone. I keep a stockpile of them in my office. I sometimes even use the book as a kind of thank-you card, mailing it to someone with a handwritten note in the cover saying, "I look forward to talking with you about this book when you've read it!"

Back in 2004, my partner at Lakeside had shared my transaction-based mindset. I shared Ferrazzi's book with him, and it affected him just as it had affected me. Because my partner and I both started changing our behavior, we were able to watch and learn from each other. We each give the other credit for helping us both make that change, and because we are the leaders of the firm, it has begun to trickle down to our employees.

Even though the change was gradual, and it was one little victory at a time, the changes began to add up: The conference behavior. The birthday calls. The way we treated the people we work with.

The transformational moment wasn't that everything changed at once; it was the realization that there was something else out there, another way of doing things.

Now I want to pay it forward to you. For the rest of this book, I want to share with you what I've learned about this *other way* of doing things—the mindset of abundance, the shift to relationships rather than transactions, the focus on caring. Of course, my education is far from over—I am still learning new things every day, and I can't wait to see what's next!

PART TWO

Engagement Is Hard Work, Not Magic

CHAPTER 4

Empower and Engage Your People

The best way to predict the future is to create it.

—PETER DRUCKER

A close cousin of the abundance-scarcity struggle for many people—particularly entrepreneurs—is the need to control. We sometimes think, "You can't do that task as well as I can," or, "It will take too long to explain it, so I may as well just do it myself." Too often, we're not open to the idea that doing something differently from the way we do things could be as good—or even better. So we don't delegate. We don't open our minds to other ways of doing things or to the possibility that somebody else might actually have a better idea than we do. We look for people to confirm what we already know to be true and what already works, rather than seeking out other possibilities and points of view.

This is a natural human tendency, so common and ingrained that it has a name: confirmation bias. Our inclination can be to seek out information that confirms our point of view. We all have our own opinions, but frequently when we encounter somebody who has a different opinion, we stop listening. We're more interested in looking for evidence that confirms our point of view rather than new information.

If I'm a conservative and watch Fox News and nothing else, I get a parade of people who agree with me. If I'm a liberal and watch MSNBC, same thing. It makes me feel comfortable, and every time somebody says something I agree with, it makes me feel smart. "See?" I say to myself. "They just proved my point!" If I turn to the other network, it just pisses me off, because people are constantly saying things I disagree with, and that makes me feel dumb. This may be an unfair characterization to use as an example, but the point is that confirmation bias is real and pervasive.

Of course, this is a simplification, but that's more or less the effect it has on your amygdala, the reptilian part of your brain where *wrong* equals *death*. As Dave Logan, John King, and Halee Fischer-Wright explain in their book, *Tribal Leadership*, we want our tribe to agree with us and reinforce our thinking. And when we don't get that agreement and reinforcement, we feel like we've been kicked out of the tribe. That feeling leads to all sorts of irrational behavior.[1]

This happens naturally, and you have to work hard to be conscious of it and overcome it. It's hard to listen objectively to someone who disagrees with you, to stand with your arms uncrossed and hear what they have to say.

In order to be open to listening to other people's points of

---

1   Dave Logan, John King, and Halee Fischer-Wright, *Tribal Leadership: Leveraging Natural Groups to Build a Thriving Organization* (New York: HarperBusiness, 2011).

view—points of view that may be contradictory to your own—you have to be willing to put your own point of view aside. You have to be willing to let go of your ego and bias.

Leaders, managers, and coworkers have to be open to knowing that they don't know everything. We have to be open to sometimes being wrong. We have to listen when people come to us and say, "This thing about the workplace isn't working so great. Let's improve it." If I as the leader set up a hierarchy in which nobody can respectfully question or argue with me or a manager, then the company is going to be limited in what it can accomplish based on the abilities of the few versus the abilities of the collective community. If we operate under the assumption that we are smarter than everybody else, that no one else can come up with something that we haven't already thought of, that nobody else's solutions are going to be as good as ours, then we negate the collective IQ of the company. There's no addition or multiplication. There's no accumulation of wisdom or ideas. There's no growth, no making things better. Everything will just stay the same.

When you empower and engage your colleagues, rather than just telling them what to do, you raise the collective IQ of the workplace. If I hire you to perform a function, it's probably because you're smart and skilled and have some experience. But if you come in on your first day and are told what to do and how to do it, then you're really

> In order to be open to listening to other people's points of view—points of view that may be contradictory to your own—you have to be willing to put your own point of view aside. You have to be willing to let go of your ego and bias.

just a continuation of what already exists. You're just another person doing the same thing. You're just an extension of what already existed.

If instead leaders say, "Here's what needs to be done. Here's some structure we employ to do it, and here's the way we've done it in the past—but I'm open to new possibilities," you are no longer just an extension of the leaders. Instead, you've compounded us. You're an addition. Now we have our IQ *plus* your IQ. Now we can collaborate and innovate and improve the work community in a more effective—and, frankly, enjoyable—manner.

In my mind, being the CEO doesn't mean that I have any more skills than any of the people I work with or that I am any smarter. In their book, *The Power of Peers*, Leon Shapiro and Leo Bottary write, "As CEO, you may not always be the smartest one in the room, but at the office, you're often treated that way because you're the ultimate decision maker."[2]

I have been known to say that the secret to great leadership is that everybody I hire is smarter than me. People think it's funny, and some of them probably think I'm kidding, but I'm not. If I'm willing to tell you that you're smarter than me, my expectation is that you'll prove me right. And chances are, if the boss tells you you're smarter than him, you're going to *want* to prove him right!

I say this because it's true and also because it's in the best interest of the company. Why would I hire somebody for their smarts and then limit them? It doesn't make any sense! Why not empower them to use the skills they were hired for?

If leadership empowers you, you're very likely to come up with a solution on how to do something better or faster or more efficiently. When you do, you get to "own" that success—which is exactly what

---

2   Leon Shapiro and Leo Bottary, *The Power of Peers* (Abingdon, UK: Routledge, 2016).

should happen. Leaders want you to have that ownership.

If we manage people, we get productivity. They'll do what we tell them or perform a task. But if we empower people, we get engagement. When you empower someone to figure something out for themselves, to be creative and discover in a way that works best for them, they have a sense of ownership over their work. They care about it. They're going to want to make it the best it can be because it "belongs" to them.

Without ownership, people are generally less motivated to work to figure things out. They have their script, their dialogue, and their rules, but without permission, they are less likely to be successful. It is highly empowering for leaders and managers to make it clear to our people that we believe they are fully capable of solving any problem they may encounter, that we are *available* as a resource if needed, but the expectation is they have the ability to act and think independently first.

We had a senior manager once come to us and ask about creating a new team to address client engagement. She asked that her team *not* include any of the executive team. Part of her thought process was that her team would feel freer or less intimidated to openly share ideas about their project within their peer group in the beginning. Then the project could be brought to the executive team for approval when completed. This process accomplished two significant outcomes: the first was a great improvement to our client engagement experience, and the other was that the *employees* completely owned the accomplishment because execs were not involved!

* * *

Empowering people goes beyond just empowering them to do certain tasks in their own way. It's about empowering people throughout the workplace, so that they feel engagement and ownership not just with their own jobs but with the company as a whole. They are empowered not just at their desks but throughout the ecosystem.

For example, if someone is to be hired, it's important for the people they're going to be working with to have input as much as is practical. If we're hiring someone for an accounting position, it would be great if a few people from the accounting department would go out to lunch with the candidate and see if they like one another. They may be spending forty-plus hours a week together from now on, and it won't be good for anyone—or business—if they simply don't like each other.

This process also empowers employees to feel some ownership over their work environment. If managers hire somebody for accounting, and a new person shows up one day in the department that you didn't know anything about—you had no say in the matter even though you're the one who's going to be working next to the person every single day—you're apt to feel a sense of powerlessness. Even though you wouldn't have made the final hiring decision, you probably would have valued being included in the process.

I also think it's meaningful to give people as much ownership over their own careers as is practically possible. One of the ways I try to stay in tune with team members on this topic is to get out to one-on-one lunches once or twice a year with everyone who works with us. (This may be impractical at larger companies, but certainly department heads and managers can figure out a way to address one-on-one attention.) At these lunches, I usually ask, "Where do you see yourself at this company in the next three to five years?" I'd say 25 percent of the time I ask that question, somebody will say, "Yeah, I've been here a couple years now, and I like what I'm doing, but when I see these people over there in that department, I think *that's* what I'm really passionate about."

"Okay," I'll say. "That's good to know. Let me talk about that with your manager if you haven't already." I then go back to the manager and say, "Hey, I just had lunch with Mary the other day. She'd really like to learn more about the technology department. Right now, she's in operations." And after talking about it, we usually end up saying, "You know what—Mary's skill set would be great in technology right now, because we have this need and that need. We can replace her in her current position with so-and-so, who's expressed an interest in operations." And much of the time, we end up making the change.

This is useful because it places people where their skills, interests, and passions are put to best use; it also sends an empowering message to everyone around her. Mary will say, "I had lunch with the CEO and told him I had an interest in working in the technology department, and six months later, I'm working in the technology department! Clearly, they really care about us."

We have several people who are doing jobs for us today that aren't even remotely related to what they were originally hired for. The company just runs better when we have the right people in the right seats. People are happier and work harder when they are doing the work they really want to do. It builds trust between managers, execs, and the employees, because questions were asked and actions were taken. It builds trust with everyone else in the company, because they know they can talk to anyone in the hierarchy, and they'll listen. The bottom line is the employees will care more.

The sense of ownership people experience if they are empowered sometimes manifests itself as behavior that indicates in small ways how and why your people care about the company. It may seem silly, but I've noticed that if someone here at our office is walking down the hallway, and there's a piece of trash on the floor, they will *always* pick it up and throw it away. It's such a small thing, but it tells you a lot about how they feel about their jobs. If they were at home, they wouldn't just let a piece of garbage sit in the hallway—and they feel the same sense of ownership and pride in their workplace that they feel in their home.

As CEO, it may be perceived by others that this is "my business," but it isn't really; it's theirs too. It's important that they feel the same pride, the same ownership, that I do. I want them to care about it and put their creativity and skills into it, because it is theirs too. Of course, there will obviously be a difference in some level of care between the owner of a business and the employees. That is just natural; after all, as the owner, I have a higher-stakes investment in the company. But they *will* care more than you'd expect—if you give them the right reasons to care.

As a leader, you can incrementally create an environment that increases employee engagement and investment in the company. This takes time and effort, and most importantly, it requires *flexibility*. It takes flexibility to help someone achieve a goal that differs from what you originally hired them for. It takes flexibility in your opinions to be open to other people's ideas and to new ways of doing things.

* * *

Empowerment is not just about delegating tasks. It's about delegating innovation and problem-solving. It's about getting people to think less like employees and more like entrepreneurs—in other words, getting people to be *intrapreneurs*. An intrapreneur is someone who works within a company but has a similar initiative-taking attitude as an entrepreneur starting their own business. Obviously, you want to create a workplace where you can cultivate intrapreneurs.

It takes a certain kind of person to be a true entrepreneur. It requires a degree of fearlessness that verges on recklessness. I definitely fall into that category: I changed my career course at age thirty-eight, threw away everything I knew, and started over with little idea of where I was actually going. There's a small percentage of the population who, like me, are unsatisfied enough that they are willing to take such an extreme step because they are looking for something more. But there's a larger group of people, especially in the coming generations, who want to express their creativity and ownership in the workplace but don't necessarily have an appetite for all the risk. These people can become intrapreneurs.

How do you engage this type of person? How do you create an office full of intrapreneurs? By empowering them, by encouraging them to question, and perhaps most importantly, by creating a safe place to fail.

CHAPTER 5

Give People a Safe Place to Fail

Your network is your net worth.

—TIM SANDERS, AUTHOR OF *LOVE IS THE KILLER APP*

Very little of what was discussed in the previous chapter is possible if you don't create a safe place for people to try new things. If I'm going to encourage you to explore and to try new things, I also have to give you the reassurance that if you fail, it's okay. You had an idea, it didn't work for whatever reason, but it's all part of you being engaged in your workplace. It's part of what I've asked you to do. This concept is true for almost any relationship we have. Parents, managers, coaches—all would inspire a more creative and growth-oriented environment with this practice.

In the workplace, it's really tough for some people to get out of the employer or employee mindset and to start thinking entrepreneurially—as if they were the business owner. An employee has to have the courage to put forth new ideas, and the leader has to have the vision to make innovation a safe transaction. People shouldn't have to be afraid that if they try a new idea and it fails—or if they propose a new process and their manager turns it down—that they are going to be punished, humiliated, or even lose their jobs.

In his book, *Creativity, Inc.*, Ed Catmull, the former president of Pixar, points out that the minute a leader doesn't make it safe for you to fail, they have stifled innovation, if not outright killed it.[3] As a result, the next good idea isn't going to come from your people easily—or if it does, they will be hesitant to step forward confidently because of the potential consequences.

In his book, Catmull explains that at Pixar, they had periodic pitch meetings where the writers, producers, and animators got together in a room and talked through ideas for a movie. Catmull had intentionally created an environment in which it was safe for someone to bring in a risky idea—and for it not to work. It was a safe place where people knew that even though some of their ideas may be failures, that didn't mean *they themselves* were failures.

Now, Catmull was managing artists and creatives, so it's obviously a whole different world from the financial services arena—or is it? One could argue that his entire industry is about creativity, so it's even more critical that the people are managed in a way that creates a safe space for failure. But I think that would be underestimating how powerful a healthy and creative environment would be in *any* industry.

As one of the leaders of a financial services company, I have a

---

3   Ed Catmull, *Creativity, Inc.: Overcoming the Unseen Forces That Stand in the Way of True Inspiration* (New York: Random House, 2014).

different set of challenges than Catmull had. One of these challenges is that financial services is generally considered a linear, left-brained business as opposed to a creative, right-brained one like filmmaking. When people think of financial services, they generally think it's all numbers and research. But the truth is, finance is a messy business because people and customer service are at the center of it—and people are messy!

Most companies—large or small—have processes, procedures, and structures for good reasons. The challenge is how the *people* who work within this structure will be managed.

When you get to the heart of it, most businesses—in any industry—deal with people, both customers and employees, which means leaders will be challenged on how to lead more creatively. And that sometimes means trying things that don't work, things that are different, things that aren't perfect.

There's an old aphorism: "Perfect is the enemy of good." If you wait for something to be perfect before you implement it or share it, you're probably going to be waiting forever. This book is a perfect example. I kept putting off writing it because I didn't think I could make it perfect. I didn't think I had learned everything that I could. I didn't think I had anything meaningful to share. So I put off writing it, wanting to write the *perfect* book, instead of just trying to write a *good* book that might give a few people some new insights. But the truth is that

> The idea that things have to be perfect in order to be useful or worthwhile or successful is limiting because most things in life aren't perfect, and what's more, they're probably not supposed to be.

even if I've written an unremarkable book that helps only ten people—or just one person—then it will absolutely have been worth it and certainly better than if I'd never written it at all, despite the fear of being judged.

The idea that things have to be perfect in order to be useful or worthwhile or successful is limiting because most things in life aren't perfect, and what's more, they're probably not supposed to be. In fact, even if something is perfect to me, it may not be perfect to you, because my definition or point of view is different from yours. Humankind's willingness to take risks and go with good, rather than hanging around and waiting for perfect, has allowed many to achieve dreams that may otherwise have never happened. Waiting for perfection could mean missing out on something really important.

At home, I am an amateur chef and cook almost every day. I love it because it is different almost every time depending on what I am making (I don't like recipes!). The process allows me to be creative and try things I just make up on the spot—and trust me, they are not all hits! But I have created some amazing dishes because I didn't get discouraged by the ones that ended up in the trash. I gave myself that permission.

It's also important, as a leader, to be open about your own failures. If you stand up in front of thirty-five people and say, "I was way off base with this idea, but you guys saved my butt, and I appreciate it," your colleagues will know that it is okay to be wrong sometimes—regardless of who you are. I think it's important to share successes *and* failures with your coworkers, friends, and even kids. We all have winners and losers, and by sharing them, we create vulnerability—which quickly leads to trust.

Of course, there are times when you as the decision maker have to make tough decisions, and sometimes that can mean overriding a popular idea. Business can't afford to fail over and over and never succeed. You can protect innovation, however, by rejecting ideas in a way that shows you still value the input of the people who bring them to you.

Making the changes people suggest or request is not always possible, whether it's an innovative new idea or a desire to work in a different role within the company, as we discussed in the last chapter. Even though I'd like to keep people engaged and implement everybody's ideas or help them move to the position they really want, it's not always the right fit for the situation. Sometimes it just won't work.

But I don't think it's productive to just say no to suggestions for change without a thoughtful response. I owe my employees a conversation: "Listen, I heard what you said. These are the reasons I don't think it is going to work out. So let's work together to figure out how we can somehow get you what you want and also be effective at getting our job done." If I'm going to pry open the oyster—if I'm going to ask people to honestly share with me what they think, what they want, what they need—I need to follow that up with respect. If I just let it go, the message being sent is that I am not really listening to what is being asked—that I don't care. By asking a question, you are setting an expectation that you care about the answer, and if you don't follow through, you are demonstrating that you don't care after all.

On the other hand, I think a leader with vision should consider saying yes at times to ideas *they* think might not work. After all, good leaders know that they are not always right. *Just because you may be the decision maker doesn't always make you right.* I believe the act of saying, "Sure, give it a try," is an empowering statement for most people to hear, and good things usually happen.

Some companies are good at sharing good news with people, but few follow up on bad news. In a safe environment, people know that their innovations may not always be successful or accepted, but they know that they will always be considered in a thoughtful and honest way. Even if the response is no (which they may not like), they will know that it's okay to go back to the drawing board. If I'm honest with you, you may be upset with me, but I haven't broken your trust.

At our firm we have tried to instill that sharing your ideas is not simply "okay" to do; it's an expectation. We want you to innovate.

Entrepreneurs are typically fearless as part of their makeup. Intrapreneurs need to be fearless too. And it may seem like a paradox, but you can truly be fearless in the workplace only if you know that you are safe. You can take risks and shoot for the stars only if you know you will be protected if you fall.

CHAPTER 6

Let Every Employee See Their Impact

*Not all of us can do great things, but we
can all do things with great love.*

—MOTHER TERESA

Empowerment goes beyond just coming up with new ideas and ways
of doing things. Employees are also empowered and engaged when
they can actually see the effect of their individual contributions to
the company—when they can see that the work they do has real
meaning. Too often, people can feel disconnected from the bigger
picture of the work a company does. Sitting at their desk, focused on
the job at hand, they may never see the final product or output, and
so they may never get a clear vision of how the work they do affects
the customer experience.

If people can't see their individual effect, they eventually feel like cogs in a machine—a machine in which they may not even understand what their cog means in the process. Nobody wants that; they want to know that what they do matters. Today's workplaces need to learn how to connect the dots for people and make the changes that allow them to see that the work they do as individuals really matters to the company and to the customer. Help them see their handprint.

> Today's workplaces need to learn how to connect the dots for people and make the changes that allow them to see that the work they do as individuals really matters to the company and to the customer.

I think the best way to relate this point is for me to cite a couple of specific examples at our workplace.

* * *

Nicole works in operations at our firm. One of her responsibilities is to open new customer accounts. She prepares the paperwork, which is very detailed and pretty lengthy—a full twelve to fifteen pages of documents for clients to sign. The data is gathered for her to enter into the computer program, and she produces the documents for customer signatures. The information needed to complete this paperwork includes personal and financial information as well as specific information about what types of investments are involved. When completed, the advisor then sits with the new client and walks them through the paperwork and signatures. Or at least that's how we *used to* do it.

Nicole probably knows every client we have, because she's entered their social security numbers, their salaries, their addresses, their birthdays, and their kids' names, among other things, into these forms. She knows everything about them, but until recently, she had never actually *seen* most of them. Her space was in the part of the office that was not client facing, so naturally, *she* was not client facing either.

When we noticed this, I thought, "Wouldn't it be meaningful for Nicole to actually connect with the client? To put a face to all the data, to this person she only knows by name, rank, and serial number? How could we give her some human contact rather than just a computer? How would that enrich her work experience?"

We decided to try making Nicole more a part of the client paperwork-signing meeting. After all, she knows it better than we do—she's the one who spends her day preparing it! More importantly, her involvement in this step establishes a more personal connection between her and the client. Then it's not just paperwork; it's a human interaction that makes the work more meaningful.

So I said to Nicole, "You know what? When we bring in a new client, why don't you come into the meeting room and walk the client through the signing?" At first Nicole was shy about this proposal, but she agreed. When the day arrived and the next new client came in, I brought her in too.

At first, Nicole was nervous. I was pushing her outside her comfort zone—but I was also making it safe for her because we talked it through ahead of time. I was excited for her because I knew that she was going to walk away from that client interaction feeling that *her* handprint was on something. She would see firsthand that she has a vital function in the process. While she may already have known that objectively, I suspected the connection would become much deeper once she'd had the chance to deal with the client directly.

This face-to-face interaction had another, somewhat unintended, positive side effect. Nicole does great work—she doesn't make very many errors—but with so much data and numbers to enter, it's completely understandable that every so often something gets transposed. Ordinarily, when this happened, my client would say to me in our meeting, "Hey, you got my address backward here." Then we'd redline it, and I'd take it back to Nicole and say, "The address was entered wrong; let's fix that in the system." And Nicole would say, "I'm sorry; I'll fix that right away." She'd feel a little bad about making a mistake, but it was no big deal.

Now, if Nicole is the one sitting with the client, and if she's the one who made the error, the client says to her directly, "My address is wrong here." Hearing that feedback directly from the client is a lot more personal than hearing it secondhand. That personal connection creates in Nicole an even deeper sense of pride in her work, and it's going to inspire her to put in that much more effort to avoid making mistakes. That sense of ownership over your role fosters an even stronger work ethic, and the quality of Nicole's work—even if it's already very high—is going to go up another notch.

Now some might say, "That's not a good use of company time. Nicole should be at her desk opening more accounts." Could Nicole get more paperwork done if she stayed at her computer instead of coming into client meetings? Sure. But look at how happy and engaged she is after the experience. Look at how the quality of her work has gone up a notch now that she's personally responsible for part of the client experience with us. When you get employees more engaged in processes, when you let them know that they're directly connected to the output, it increases ownership of the work, and the quality of their work goes up.

Making these changes to how things operate is hard work, but it's worth it. We are constantly looking for ways to increase employee engagement, and seeing how we are able to improve Nicole's level of job satisfaction inspired us to figure out how to make more of these changes in other areas of the business. And the more we focus on making these changes, the more we get to see *our* own handprint— our own influence as leaders of this company.

While all this can make the workplace more enjoyable and productive for employees, it can have the same effect for the leaders. As CEO, it's exciting for me and the other leadership to constantly be working on ways to shape our evolving company. As a result, that involvement makes *me* much more engaged too.

It doesn't matter what position you have in the company; if you know that what you do matters, you're going to care about it, and you're going to care about the person you're helping on the other end. It's easier to care about a living, breathing, flesh-and-blood human being sitting across the table from you than to care about a bunch of numbers on a piece of paper, and that level of care is going to make you work harder, work better, and find more meaning in your work.

* * *

Kelly is one of our longest-term employees. She's been with the company since just a few years after we started. Kelly started out as a receptionist, and around that time we started working with a new client named Joe. Joe was a retired business owner, very personable and easygoing. He would sit in the reception area, and he and Kelly would talk about this and that—really just small talk. Joe and Kelly eventually became such good friends that Joe would stop by the office without even needing to see me. He would come by just to talk to Kelly and have a cup of tea with her.

Eventually we promoted Kelly to a more senior position in the company. When Joe came in and found Amanda, Kelly's successor, at her desk, he said, "What happened to Kelly?" Amanda explained that Kelly had been promoted. Joe was thrilled for her—and then he went right back to chitchatting—sitting in the reception area and talking and having tea with Amanda.

Now, fast-forward to 2018. Amanda has also been promoted to a more senior position—and Joe still comes in and says to the new receptionist, "Hey, tell Amanda and Kelly to come out; I want to show them pictures from my vacation!" And they can't wait to see him! How much more connected to the end user do you get than that type of interaction?

Last year, Kelly lost her mother, and when Joe found out, he sent her a heartfelt card that brought her to tears. She now has it thumbtacked up at her desk. Does Kelly feel that connected to *every* client at Lakeside? Of course not. But that personal connection, knowing that there are real people like Joe on the other end of the relationship, certainly helps her find meaning in the work she does sitting at her desk.

Business is always a two-way street. There's the company on one end of that street, and at the other end is the client. It's important to let people see that their work matters on both ends—that it matters to the company *and* to the client. Let people see how their individual contribution has a direct effect on the person at the other end of the relationship.

It's misguided for us to tell people only how the work they do affects the company. We'll say, "Let us show you that your job is critical by showing you how it's connected to our revenues and our bottom line." That's important, of course, but how much greater would the effect be if a leader stood up at a company meeting and said, "Hey, do you remember the account we opened last week? Here's how that client is doing and how thankful they are for the work you did." Or if I said, "Hey, everybody, Joe called and wanted us all to know what a great job Kelly did and that the advice she gave him about his grandson was really meaningful."

If somebody's work has an effect in terms of a personal relationship, that makes it even more tangible and meaningful, and that can have a huge effect on how somebody feels about their job. The truth is, not every job is an exciting and stimulating joyride. It takes a lot of little tasks to make a company run, and some of those jobs are less interesting than others, but they are still absolutely critical. For all our talk about people wanting to find their dream job, their passion, those critical but uninteresting jobs still have to get done—but you can still be passionate about them.

How can you make an employee passionate about something objectively boring, like data entry? By showing them how their data entry is part of this account, which is connected to this human being, and by showing them how it has made a difference in that human being's life. Let them foster those personal relationships, as Kelly and Amanda did with Joe.

* * *

The problem of people feeling disconnected from their work is not a new one. There have always been people who have felt like their jobs didn't really have meaning and didn't really matter—like me at the Chicago Board of Trade for so many years. Thirty years ago, people didn't say anything about these topics. These feelings went unspoken. Today, however, the unspoken is being spoken, and that has a lot to do with a whole new generation of people coming into the workplace: millennials.

CHAPTER 7

Love Your Millennials

What we often consider unsolvable is just a crisis
waiting for a new generation of leaders.

**—REX MILLER, MABEL CASEY, AND MARK KONCHAR , AUTHORS
OF *CHANGE YOUR SPACE, CHANGE YOUR CULTURE***

Millennialism is a hot topic right now, and a lot of people are hungry
for answers. A new generation has entered the workforce and is
changing the workplace.

Many leaders can feel frustrated when it comes to dealing with
millennials, and one of the biggest problems is retention. It's expensive
for a firm to acquire and train new hires, and the business interrup-
tion of starting from square one with new people can be expensive as
well. Ironically, I don't think retention is really the problem by itself
as much as it is a result of the larger problem: that we don't fully
understand this new employment landscape yet.

If you look at many of today's workplaces, they aren't really a reflection of the people who work there anymore. In the last several decades, the composition of the employees has changed—as you would expect. Retirees leave the workforce, and graduates enter it. Some research predicts that by 2030, there may be as many as 75 percent of workers in the millennial age group (defined as those born between approximately 1981 and 1996).

It would be logical, therefore, to expect that in order to successfully engage a completely new workforce, you will need a new and improved set of tools: new office designs to enable new workflows, technology, and reverse mentoring, to name a few.

Obviously, one of the big differences between my generation and the younger ones (millennial and X) is communication and the use of technology. Smartphones and social media have drastically changed the landscape, transforming how millennials—and all of us—communicate and interact with the world. Thirty years ago, we communicated differently. We didn't have cell phones, and the internet was in its infancy. As a result, we weren't always checking in and checking up on people. Today, we communicate in real time. I wouldn't necessarily say the conversations are more meaningful; it's just that the frequency is different. The level of expectation and response time has changed.

Today we have constant access to one another, and while that is convenient in many ways, it also has its challenges. Communication used to be a straight line from one person to another. Now we have so many modes of communication—calling, texting, emailing, social media, messaging apps—that instead of a straight line, we have a web. That's how we communicate in our personal lives, and it has become second nature for many. Because of this shift, it would be unreasonable and impractical to ask someone to come to work and communicate differently than they do in the rest of their lives.

Sociologically, we are evolving. It would be unwise not to try creating a work environment that parallels that evolution. Effective leaders can't expect people to come to work and completely change how the rest of the world has trained them to behave, communicate, and interact.

Like many people of my generation, I can quickly get frustrated whenever I have to learn a new technology. It's not that I don't want to use the technology, but learning *how* to use it doesn't come as easy for me. Millennials, for the most part, are comfortable with new devices and applications. They're able to figure them out quickly because they grew up with a smartphone in their hand; it's second nature to them. Boomers can learn to use these new tools, but many of us have a slightly less intuitive approach because it's relatively "new" to us.

Millennials tend to be three- or four-device people. They're on their computers and their phones at the same time, in multiple tabs and using multiple programs, switching back and forth faster than *my* brain can process. This has its upsides and its downsides. On one hand, this inherent ability to multitask can be really good for productivity. On the other hand, you can get distracted and be less productive by having that many things going on. This can vary from one person to another, but I don't think it's fair to assume that multitasking necessarily equals distraction.

Overall, it would be wise for us to better understand how social media networks affect businesses in today's world. In any business, if you don't give a customer good service, there will be a reaction. That customer will tell their friends, and word will spread. That has always been the case, but today it is hugely amplified by social media, Yelp, and so on. This kind of far-reaching ability to communicate puts pressure on the provider of the service or product to do whatever they can to give the consumer the best value—as it should be.

Of course, it shouldn't matter that it's easy for somebody to broadcast their experience; you should be treating them the same way no matter what. But the reality is that today, if you don't execute for the customer, a lot more people are going to know about it a lot faster than they used to. Today's communication platforms have increased our accountability and raised the standard to which we are held. Alternatively, these mediums can be powerful ways to express all the things that our businesses do well if leveraged correctly.

Millennials are more familiar and comfortable with these platforms than most baby boomers will ever be. As an employer, however, this gives me the opportunity to say to my colleagues, "Let's figure out a way that between your comfort level with technology and your skill set, we can work together to create a better customer experience *and* a better workplace and employee experience." That's very different from just saying, "Get off Facebook and get back to work!"

As parents and grandparents, we can see that the new generation

While the concept of mentoring is not a new idea, reverse mentoring has been gaining popularity as a strategy to bridge the gap in many areas in a changing workforce.

is different, that they communicate differently, and so we adapt the way we parent. Why is it so hard to see that the same change should happen in the workplace? Why would we not try to adapt the workplace to the changing world?

The concept of reverse mentoring is a great option for connecting millennials in a more meaningful way in the workplace. Matching up junior teammates and having them "teach" technology to the more senior (generally older) people is just one example. While the concept of mentoring is not a new idea, reverse mentoring has been gaining popularity as a strategy to bridge the gap in many areas in a changing workforce. Other benefits include building confidence and leadership skills for the younger mentors as well as creating mutual respect between the generations. Ultimately, one way or another, these are our future leaders.

* * *

Technology has transformed our world, but the changes millennials want to bring to the workplace go beyond technological platforms. So what do millennials want? The best way to find that out is to ask them.

One of our responsibilities as leaders is to make it clear to our younger employees and colleagues that we're willing to listen to them. If there is something in the workplace that is not working so great or that you think could work better, let's talk about it. Instead of packing your bags, fight for the kind of workplace you want because *you* are the future leaders.

This is what we did at Lakeside. We took an informal survey of the millennials in our office, and we found that a few points came up consistently. Millennials need to know that we want their ideas. They need to know that what they do matters. They think of a job more as a calling. They feel that both sides of the employer-employee equation are replaceable. They want to know that it's safe to fail. They don't want to be underestimated or treated like the youngest person in the room. They prefer a clear career path. They want a mix of hands-on and hands-off management. They need high energy and stimulation.

Many of these expectations may sound familiar—and they should. Most of us have the same expectations wherever we work. What I have learned is that there are really not many differences between what the generations want, just in the way they demand it—not disrespectfully but more vocally.

In general, millennials are much more honest about their feelings and much more matter of fact. Most would readily change jobs if they are not getting the validation or acknowledgment that they need. It's not about getting a pat on the back if it's unwarranted; millennials just want to be acknowledged for the work they're doing and the contributions they're making. Of course, everybody wants this acknowledgment—and everybody should get it—but millennials are more vocal about it.

One of the other common responses in our survey was that millennials are sensitive to being underestimated. A millennial doesn't want to be treated like the youngest one in the room—even if they often are. They may not have an important title or much experience yet—so how do I, as a leader, make them feel like an equal contributor? By treating them like one, regardless of the differences in our paychecks and titles. That might not bridge the gap completely, but it will certainly help them from feeling like they have nothing to contribute.

Occasionally, when we're having a meeting, I'll look to the youngest person in the room or to someone who hasn't really spoken up and ask, "Well, what do *you* think?" This sometimes may cause an awkward moment as it was unexpected, but I think it's important to give them the space to answer—to let it percolate a bit!

A couple of interesting dynamics happen during this interaction. First, the person probably thinks, "Wow, leadership actually cares what I think!" The second is that they realize they're going to get called on to contribute—that they're going to be asked what they think—so they're going to start thinking things through a lot more. They'll be more prepared at the next meeting.

Unfortunately, I have seen a common reaction from managers

who think, "What can that twenty-five-year-old add to the discussion? He's only been in the business a couple of years." Perhaps there is *some* practical truth to that, but that person is going to struggle to develop professionally if I am always saying he or she needs to have more experience, needs to be older, needs to have been here longer— and not making clear what "more," "older," and "longer" mean!

Instead, I could accelerate their growth by encouraging them to contribute, by asking what they think—and then listening. I may walk back to my office thinking, "Well, in this case, their input wasn't that useful." But even if it wasn't immediately helpful in resolving the issue being discussed, it's useful in another way: it nourishes them and helps them grow. This means they'll become more useful in the company more quickly than they would have if we had not provided that environment.

Moreover, it's a succession plan! How are we going to transition our businesses to the next generation if we don't mentor them and allow them to develop and flourish? The only way we'll be able to pass this company on successfully to the next generation is if they become as good at marketing, networking, and growing the business as we were. So it's better to start that process now, when they're in their twenties and thirties, than ten years from now when *I'm* ready to retire.

We are always looking for ways to mentor the next generation. We believe the mentoring process is as good for the giver as it is for the receiver. An example of this mutually beneficial mentoring can be seen in the following example.

As a financial services company, it is important for us to have relationships with certified public accountants (CPAs), who are good referral sources for us. Historically, the principals of the respective firms are the ones that spend the most time together, but we began feeling like this approach was missing an opportunity. Recently, we've started having periodic networking events with a somewhat different focus.

Before the events, the principals meet to discuss which of their teams and how many people will attend the networking social. Generally, what we try to accomplish is matching up age groups as much as possible (millennials, Generation X, boomers) to allow and encourage these age groups to grow their relationships—personal and strategic.

After one of these events, we challenge the young people to take action to further develop their new relationship. We encourage them to get new contacts out in a one-on-one situation that push their boundaries a bit and ultimately help them grow. I think it's the right thing to do, and furthermore, it's what millennials are telling us they want and need in their professional lives.

Thirty years ago, the way we kept people around was mostly compensation—we paid them more. We gave them more vacation days or better benefits. We battled the competition by outbidding them for talented employees. Today, money alone isn't going to keep people around. The conversation about this topic is moving to various forms of compensation beyond just the paycheck. Compensation means satisfaction, ownership, meaning, and engagement—and it means the opportunity to continue growing and developing as a professional.

* * *

Some people might still be thinking, "Why should I put all this work into keeping these millennials around? They're just too fickle!" I'd argue that fickle is actually the opposite of what millennials truly are. Someone's willingness to change jobs fourteen times in their career in order to find something that makes them happy shows a pretty dedicated focus to seeking out a passion—and the right place to pursue that passion. Instead of treating it as a problem, we should be asking, "How do we harness that?"

Let's eliminate some of the barriers. Let's take this dedication and passion they have and motivate them to refocus it on their jobs and on what they can do to make the company better. It's a powerful engine that drives someone to uproot themselves fourteen times and move to different departments, different companies, different cities. If we can harness that and focus it on something productive and stable and gratifying, then we've really got something that could change the game.

CHAPTER 8

Game Changers

What we often consider to be unsolvable is just a crisis waiting for a new generation of leaders.

—REX MILLER, MABEL CASEY, AND MARK KONCHAR, AUTHORS OF *CHANGE YOUR SPACE, CHANGE YOUR CULTURE*

In *The Power of Peers*, Leo Bottary and Leon Shapiro write that, in general, when a boss asks a question, the employee answers. However, in a group of peers—in a group of CEOs, say—one CEO, instead of answering another's questions, will question his or her answers. This type of collaborative and healthy interaction has a number of organizational benefits if properly implemented. Clear communication that makes honest and respectful questioning safe and welcome would go a long way to create engagement—and probably improvement—regardless of age or title. I want the same thing to happen with my millennial workforce. If all they are doing is answering my questions, I'm just getting my own view validated over and over, and nobody grows from that. Instead, I need to let them know that it's okay to question my answers.

Millennials are willing to challenge authority; in return, authority should be willing to allow that to happen in a productive, healthy environment. If done properly, this challenges the old guard to think differently without being intimidated or offended. The question is, How are today's leaders going to respond to these challenges? Are we going to be offended or intimidated? Or are we going to do a better job listening in order to embrace the new generation and the changes they bring?

Wait a minute, you may be thinking. Are you telling me I have to change my workplace to accommodate a new generation of employees?

My answer is, "Of course!"

I hear people complain about how millennials want things to be different. Don't you think things should be different than they were thirty years ago? Shouldn't the workplace evolve the same way that people have evolved?

You don't have to remake your entire company. But you do have to be aware that it's different—and I think, in many ways, it's better. Too many people, of all generations, are so worried about change and what it will mean (we all hate the unknown!) that they won't slow down and say, "Wait a minute; you make some good points. Let's explore that some more." Fear of change can often cloud our vision as to better ways to make our worlds work.

I was having lunch with a friend recently, and he said he'd realized that things become a lot clearer when you stop looking at situations as always "either/or." Some situations are not either/or; sometimes, they're "and."

This is a big thought shift, especially for people of my generation who are often, for lack of a better phrase, stuck in their ways.

It's almost ingrained in us sometimes to think something has to be an "either/or" situation rather than an "and" scenario. But it's not always a matter of either the old way or the new way. Sometimes you don't have to discard *all* the old ideas in order to start with some new ones. In fact, you can sometimes create a unique combination of both, which could even work better than the other two options on their own!

This can be a particularly difficult thought shift for entrepreneurs who have created successful businesses. If you started a company, grew it from nothing, and made all your own decisions so far, this mindset of not welcoming others' ideas can be limiting, if not potentially devastating, for your company's future. Yes, you deserve credit for having a successful idea, one you executed well, but you can't stop there. You can't just say, "Okay, let's just keep doing the same thing over and over; I'm sure it will continue to be successful." It probably won't.

There is a Chinese proverb that says roughly, "The longer you stand in the same place, the less you will see," which I think sums up my point quite eloquently.

I find it ironic that entrepreneurs—who have built their businesses by pushing boundaries, breaking rules, and changing the game—would be the ones to stand by such a restrictive

> My (boomer) generation needs to do a much better job of realizing that change is necessary and normal and that it is actually useful and productive to receive input from the millennial workforce.

mindset. Trying new stuff and facing challenges is what got you where you are; why would you be offended or intimidated by somebody who wants to do the very same thing just because they're younger than you? That's an attitude of, "Do as I say, not as I do," and that will get you *somewhere*, but not nearly where you *could* be.

My (boomer) generation needs to do a much better job of realizing that change is necessary and normal and that it is actually useful and productive to receive input from the millennial workforce. That requires some honesty as well as humility. It sometimes requires the ability to swallow one's ego. However, it goes both ways. Members of the next generation have to commit to honesty and check their egos at the door equally. Boomers didn't arrive here on luck alone; they learned a thing or two through their years of experience. Both sides need to work together to create an environment that's the best of both worlds. My generation brought a lot of good stuff to the workplace, and we don't have to throw all of it away. We just have to figure out an intelligent way to incorporate all the new things that are available.

What we could have now, in the union of these two generations, is an amazing opportunity to forge a new way of working and create a new type of workplace. Our attitude shouldn't be, *Oh no, I* have *to change my workplace to accommodate millennials*. A healthier response should be, *I get to innovate and change my workplace, because the opportunities millennials will allow me to have are endless.*

Honestly, I couldn't be more excited about the future. I truly look forward to learning what someone thirty years my junior can teach me about the way I'm doing things. That's how we multiply the collective IQ of the workplace. Why would you ignore someone's ability to contribute? Once again, it's about people *supplementing* one another rather than one simply *being an extension* of the other.

Instead of telling my team, "We've got this problem, and I can't fix it. We've tried, and we can't do it, so let's just learn to live with it," we should be saying, "I haven't been able to figure out a solution for this. Anybody got any ideas?" The conversation that approach stimulates and the energy it creates are really cool; plus, it's much more likely that together, we'll solve the problem! Moreover, this is exactly what millennials are looking for. They want that engagement. They want to be included. They don't want to be the children being told what to do by the adults. They yearn to be an equal participant and to be respected as one.

You may have noticed that much of what we're talking about here—the changes we need to make to the workplace to embrace the wants and needs of millennials—is what I have detailed in previous chapters. In return, we can expect them to more readily embrace where they work and what they are contributing. Opening ourselves up to new ideas; empowering and engaging our employees; letting all of our workers see their influence; and acknowledging their accomplishments, collaborating, listening, and being flexible are changes we should be making to make workplaces better.

The truth is, we're all more alike than we are different. We're headed to a similar destination, and we have similar needs. The optics are just way more apparent now than they were before. A lot of what millennials are looking for isn't exactly new; there probably isn't as much revolutionary thought around the employer-employee relationship as people think there is. Across our interviews with our millennials, I never really heard anything I didn't agree with: "I want to be known for having left a mark on the business." "I want to be able to show that I effected some change." "I want to know that what I do matters." I thought the same things when I was their age; I just didn't talk about it.

The big difference is that this new generation is more honest and vocal than the previous one. Thirty years ago, people had these same needs, but they didn't speak up. That just wasn't done. Some people might argue that's better—that millennials should simply put up with things they don't like. I disagree. I don't believe people should

> I don't believe people should have to endure workplace situations that make them miserable; I think that's limiting.

have to endure workplace situations that make them miserable; I think that's limiting.

The fact is, nobody has ever wanted work to be a chore. Millennials are just much more candid about wanting a job that is more than just a job—one in which they can truly invest themselves. They're saying, "I want to find a job that I care about and go to a place where I *want* to be, rather than a place I *have* to be."

I don't think that's any different than what I wanted or what my dad wanted. We just didn't discuss it. My dad was in the insurance business for a while, and after that, the steel business, and I can't remember him ever coming home and saying, "I can't wait to go to work tomorrow!" It was definitely a chore—an obligation, rather than an opportunity. He may have liked what he did for a living, but he didn't like going to work. This was probably because of the environment—because if the atmosphere of the workplace wasn't good, it had the ability to reduce the enjoyment factor of any job.

Change is also occurring because we're allowing children to be self-directed earlier and earlier, to choose what they want to do and how they like to play. Kids don't grow up and automatically go into the same professions as their parents anymore. Today, you don't have to do exactly what your parents planned out for you; you're encouraged to forge your own path.

This is happening all over the world, thanks to social media. Now young people have access to all the opportunities out there.

They're not limited by what they see their parents or their friends' parents doing. Instead, they have a much broader view of the world. They are empowered by the access to information, in all its iterations: personal, professional, cultural, political, legal, and so on. Why wouldn't they grow up more self-directed, more willing to pursue their passions, and more outspoken about what they want? That's part of the reason the millennial generation is the "follow your bliss" generation. For millennials, work is more than just a job; it is connected to who they are as people.

In 1984, Apple introduced its Macintosh personal computer with a Super Bowl ad that has now become famous. Inspired by George Orwell's *Nineteen Eighty-Four*, the ad shows a young woman carrying a hammer—representing Apple and the Macintosh computer—charging through a dystopian world in which everyone looks the same and smashing through the screen that is brainwashing the masses with propaganda. The ad was hugely successful, and it changed the way companies advertised and appealed to consumers.

In his book *Start With Why*, Simon Sinek explains that with this ad, the marketing tactic shifted from advertisements saying, "I have something really cool, and you should buy it," to saying, "Hey, do you want to be a part of a movement? Do you want to be different and change things? Well, I can help you." Now, if I buy into that kind of thinking, if I want to be part of a movement, I don't care what you're selling me; I'm buying it. And in the 1980s, this is exactly the kind of thinking that was taking place—people wanted to be part of a movement. Apple saw that and said, "Wait a minute. People are changing the way they think. We'd better be able to change the way we communicate."

This shift occurred in 1987, which is just after the first millennials were born. They grew up in this new excitement of wanting to be part of a movement and feeling compelled to make a difference. Now, as they have become adults and entered the workplace, millennials want to have purpose. They don't just want to go to work to pay their bills; they want the work they do to make a positive difference in the world.

We use the phrase *game changer* to describe a person or thing that is really making a difference in the world. It is undoubtedly meant as a positive term. And yet many people are so afraid of change. I challenge the leaders of my generation to be game changers themselves by welcoming with open arms the next generation of game changers.

CHAPTER 9

Treat People Like Adults, and They'll Act Like Adults

My job as a leader is to create space
for learning moments.

—MICHAEL BUNGAY STANIER

As a parent, I made sure my kids grew up with a sensible number of rules and structure. They were expected to live within these rules until they were capable of creating their own structure and making (mostly) well-informed decisions. But even with kids, if you have *too* many rules in place, then their ability to grow, make mistakes, learn, and become better decision-makers may get compromised.

If you treat a child like a child forever, he or she will have a more difficult time transitioning into a mature adult. Successful parenting, on the other hand, accelerates the growth of children's skill sets, gives them more confidence, and makes them less afraid to fail.

Leaders and managers must be aware that while a certain hierarchy exists in the organizational chart, the temptation to micromanage that hierarchy along the way can be counterproductive.

Similarly, in the workplace, leaders and managers must be aware that while a certain hierarchy exists in the organizational chart, the temptation to micromanage that hierarchy along the way can be counterproductive. In a sense, we can inadvertently create an unhealthy "parent-child" relationship with employees.

One of the unintended outcomes that can come from too many or too rigid rules is they can cause a lack of productivity and engagement. Another one of the more limiting issues is that without appropriate flexibility, employee creativity and innovation can be stifled.

At our company, we have generally observed that when the personality of the work environment becomes inflexible and overly managed, then this parent-child dynamic can be created between employees and managers. This is harmful in several ways—some of which are not so obvious.

In the workplace, a parent-child dynamic, versus a healthier peer-peer relationship, can change the way people feel about their ability to move about the office and to freely create and innovate. The danger is that for some people, their focus can be so intent on following rules that pushing boundaries—even in a healthy manner— is no longer an option; they are simply too afraid of breaking the rules.

Specifically, in the case of millennials (as mentioned in previous chapters), this type of work environment can exacerbate their frustration with being treated like the youngest one in the room. But, according to our informal survey, being chronologically the youngest isn't the problem; the problem is being automatically discounted ability wise simply based on age.

To complicate matters, the subtlety of this dynamic goes even deeper. As the leader of an organization, aside from wanting to grow a successful business, ideally I would really want my colleagues to enjoy and be fulfilled by where they work and what they do. As employees, there is an understandable desire to be appreciated for their contributions. The tricky thing here is the optics.

A person in authority may show approval or disapproval for the work of someone who reports to them. This is a healthy and necessary part of the workplace feedback loop. The balance is to be able to deliver the feedback, criticism, and kudos in a peer-to-peer tone rather than a superior-inferior—that is, parent-child—tone. Specifically, when the feedback is more critical in nature, it can be challenging to deliver the words in a way that is about the *work* itself and not about the *person*.

In *Creativity, Inc.*, Ed Catmull discusses in some detail the difference in the way an employee engages when they feel personally judged for a mistake rather than simply the act of making a mistake: the former is internalized, the latter noninvasive. The corollary that Catmull refers to in his book is that this dynamic, if properly executed, can make the workplace a much safer place to fail.

Earlier in this chapter we discussed the need for structure to be combined with the freedom to explore. This can be a tough environment to get just right, but it helps if we understand the distinction between having rules to provide order rather than rules to control behavior. A simple example of a rule to provide order may be something such as, Don't leave confidential client documents on your desk when we have visitors in the office. An example of a rule to control behavior may be found in our experiment with our employee sick-day policy.

We have observed and read about companies recently who did away with the typical sick-day policy of so many days per year and a use-it-or-lose-it structure. From our point of view, it seemed rather ridiculous to tell responsible adults how often they could be sick and that we would keep score. Like some other firms, we believed that if we allowed employees to be responsible for their own behavior on topics like this, they would perform responsibly.

As a result, we decided to no longer track sick days. Our policy is that if you're sick, stay home. If your kid's sick, stay home. If your husband's sick and you need to take care of him, stay home. Just let people know whether you're available via email, and if you're not, no problem; just say so. If you are, then we'll email you as projects arise throughout the workday.

Now wait a minute, you may be thinking. *If we did that, nobody would ever show up for work! Everybody's going to be "sick" every day!* Well, I can tell you—in practice, that's not what happened. When we implemented this policy, there was virtually no change at all in the number of sick days our employees took. In fact, with the exception of a few anomalies for extenuating circumstances, the number of sick days used actually decreased!

Of course, there are some practical limitations that you have to have in place to deter bad behavior or people taking advantage of the system. You have to get the work done, after all. But just loosening the tether a little bit lets people know that you trust them, you believe in them, and you have faith that they will behave like the responsible adults they are.

With this policy, people don't have to stress out when they are sick, or when their kids are sick, or when they just really need to take a day off in order to be more productive throughout the rest of the week. They can think, I don't have to go to work because I know that it's okay if I work from home today. I know I'm not going to get any blowback from my manager for working remotely instead of coming in to the office when I'm not feeling well.

That permission is a critical part of engagement with employees, and especially millennials. I certainly would have appreciated it as an employee years ago, but it just wasn't an option. Either you came to work, or you used up one of your ten sick days, and once you used those up, your pay was docked.

Of course, this sick-day policy might not work at *every* company. But as an executive team, we felt comfortable making this change at Lakeside because we felt that we had done enough work on the culture and environment that people actually *wanted* to come to work. If we hadn't done a good enough job culturally, then we would be worried about people calling in sick just because they don't want to come to the office. But we think we've created an environment where people really enjoy coming in—to the point where they won't take a sick day unless they really need one.

Of course, some rules and protocol are necessary in any workplace. But if you look at some of the extensive rules in employee handbooks, you think, Really? If we're hiring people who would do that, then this employee handbook isn't going to fix the problem. We need to hire different people.

If you are hiring good people and they are behaving badly, then you have to take a hard and honest look at the culture you have created.

At the end of the day, if you treat good people like adults, they'll act like adults. If you give them responsibilities, they'll be responsible. If you hire people you trust, you should trust them, and they will live up to that trust.

Similar to the other rules that are designed to control behavior, telling somebody how to behave all the time is treating that person like a child, not an adult. And that will almost inevitably lead to stunting the ability of that individual to be the best he or she can be. If you marginalize or patronize someone, they will probably become resentful, and then they will fail to learn and grow because you have shown them that you don't believe in them.

Empowering people, giving them a safe place to innovate and fail and innovate again, letting them see their influence, embracing your game-changing millennials—all of these actions are part of treating people like adults, and we have seen that they each have a positive effect. They will push themselves, they will innovate, they will creatively solve problems—and they will go above and beyond for you, for themselves, and for your company.

CHAPTER 10

It's Not Just the Words

Most people don't listen with the intent to
understand; they listen with the intent to reply.

—STEPHEN R. COVEY

As you could probably guess, I hate the word *boss* as much as I hate
the word *employee*. I feel it can create an automatic barrier between
the people I work with and myself. If we are simply *colleagues*, it
makes the relationship much more productive.

However, socially and psychologically, the title of CEO carries
some weight. Even though I might not feel like I deserve any
different or special treatment just because of my job title—I have to
acknowledge that the tendency exists. While it might not matter to
me that I'm the CEO, I must realize that other people may perceive
me differently.

When you are the CEO, no matter how friendly and approachable you are, your words and actions carry a significant weight. It's like having a loaded gun in your hand. You have to be aware of the effect your words and actions have on the people you work with. This "weight" can work for you *and* against you, so just being aware is the first step.

> No matter how approachable a CEO is, no matter how friendly, no matter how hard they work to deemphasize the hierarchy and make it clear that everyone is equally important, a CEO's words will always have more influence.

Let me illustrate with a simple example.

Whenever we get a new receptionist, it takes them a little while to learn how the phone system works. Recently, our newest receptionist received a call from one of our big clients. The client was upset about something important, and the receptionist, still learning the ropes, rerouted the call to the wrong place.

Now, our administrative staff doesn't report to me directly; they report to our operations manager. If the ops manager says, "Hey, I understand you had a problem routing a call. Are you up for some training on the phone system?" it would certainly carry some weight. But it's an entirely different situation if I walk up to the receptionist and ask, "What happened?" Even if I don't say it angrily, those words will weigh ten times as much as the manager's.

No matter how approachable a CEO is, no matter how friendly, no matter how hard they work to deemphasize the hierarchy and make it clear that everyone is equally important, a CEO's words will always have more influence. So when a CEO, manager, or any leader calls out a mistake, it emphasizes the problem. That's why when something goes wrong, I always try to let the person's direct manager address it.

However, the reverse is also true: when a CEO delivers good news or a compliment on a job well done, it can be powerful. Studies have shown time and again that positive reinforcement is much more effective than negative reinforcement. Instead of using the weight of your words directly as CEO to punish people when they make mistakes, *do* use them directly to praise people when they do well.

Of course, there are times when negative feedback is necessary from the top, but I believe you should use this approach sparingly. Think things through before you speak. I sometimes have to swallow frustrations, because if the words leave my brain and come out of my mouth, I know they could do significant damage. That means I can't always tell a person exactly what I think. However, if I understand the interpersonal dynamic, then I can express my frustration in a way that's actually constructive.

You could make the person feel ashamed and send them home feeling bad about themselves for an error that probably wasn't intentional, or you could turn the problem into an opportunity. In the past, I've done the latter by expressing a willingness to coach or mentor a colleague who was struggling. In so doing, I've turned a negative into a huge positive. When you flip something 180 degrees, it can make a moment unforgettable. You create a memorable learning experience and also strengthen your relationship with that person as well as strengthen that person's relationship with their job.

If negative feedback should be used sparingly, the opposite is true for positive reinforcement: be appropriately generous. If the people you work with say, "The CEO or manager took time out to say this, or to send me this handwritten note, or to call me on my birthday," I assure you the effect in the workplace will be palpable.

Even the wording of compliments can provide an opportunity for more meaningful moments. I can say, "Good job," but it's infinitely more empowering if I say, "Good job, and here's why."

Additionally, always beware of the following: "Good job, but …" Even if you put a nice big pause after the "Good job," rest assured that all the other person hears is the "but," negating your well-intentioned compliment. Yes, there are circumstances where somebody did a good job *but*. That's when you find a way to convey that improvements can be made without negating the compliment. You might say something like, "Awesome job. Here is what worked really, really well. And on *this* part, I think we can really bring it up to the next level." The simplest way to "avoid the but" is to just save the feedback for another time.

While it may be true that a CEO's words weigh the most, an awareness of the full effect of communication—regardless of job title—should be a priority. Even if it's your peer who made a mistake, instead of saying, "Oh man, you really screwed that up," you can say, "Hey, I noticed this was a little off. Let's look at it together." Then it becomes an opportunity to collaborate and deepen that relationship.

As the leader, it's up to you to spread this kind of communication throughout the company. You set the bar for everyone else. Having managers and directors on the same philosophical page is incredibly important; only then will you have consistency across the entire ecosystem of the workplace.

As a leader of any type, it is your responsibility to model the right way to behave, whether it's at work, home, or out in the community. How do you act toward the people who report to you? Children? Friends? That's how you are training your mangers; they will act similarly toward the people who report to them, deploying the same habits and practices. As Dave Logan, John King, and Halee

Fischer-Wright say in their book, *Tribal Leadership*, the elders in the tribe will mimic the behavior of the chief.

As CEO, you're always going to carry authority, whether you want to or not. But you can dial that up or down depending upon what is going on around you. There's a common mindset that as CEO, you're part security guard and part parent. I think the mindset should be, "I'm working with thirty-five colleagues and mates, so let's see what we can do today." Of course, you can't have total chaos. But I believe we can and should deemphasize the hierarchical chart, encouraging a more peer-to-peer environment in the workplace. As the leader, I'm the one who sets the tone for that.

This can be done partly through how you speak to people and also through your physical actions, awareness of your surroundings, and body language. Start with your private office. My partner and I have a space separated from the rest of the office, but the walls are all glass. There are no thrones, nothing ostentatious, and the door is almost always open. We wanted it to feel open and approachable.

This consciousness goes beyond the design of the space and spills into how you use it. When someone comes into my office, I am usually friendly and welcoming, while also being aware of the power differential. And when I am sometimes not at my best, I know I have built up enough trust from previous interactions to make up for my bad day.

Also, I am acutely conscious of the message that my physical space sends. If I'm in the big chair and the other person is in a little chair in front of the desk, that indicates a certain power dynamic. Sitting at a round table versus a rectangular one and the position of your chair and your posture (among about a thousand other examples!) are all subtle messages you are sending during an interaction.

I am a six-foot-four-inch, 240-pound man, and it can be hard sometimes to not appear intimidating, but sometimes it's crucial to embody your physical authority—to loom large and take up space. At other times, it's best to *not* be standing over someone or behind the desk, to say instead, "Let's sit down on these lounge chairs in the middle of the room." Or, "Let's go out into the kitchen area to grab a coffee and talk." By doing that, you can change the physical and personal dynamic from boss-employee to friend, colleague, confidante, or whatever role you choose.

Regardless of your physical attributes, how you interact with your surroundings plays a huge role in the way people perceive you—and being aware of these subtleties is critical.

Going back to my comments about round tables versus rectangles, allow me to dig a little deeper into this psychology. Let's say you have a conference room with two chairs at each end of a long table and eight chairs along each side. There are different power positions at that table. The power position at the head of the table says, "I'm in charge of this meeting. The buck stops with me." The other power position around a board room table is the middle seat along the sides. The message that sends is, "I'm in charge, but I'm flexible and approachable." That brand of power is more passive than absolute.

You can decide which position to be in depending on context. If it's a meeting where you want everybody to contribute equally, don't put yourself in the physical position that says, "I'm in charge, and I'm going to tell everyone what to do." There is a time and a place for that, but be sure you are conscious of when you choose to use it. I've actually switched chairs in the middle of a meeting before, depending on what was happening and what we wanted to accomplish!

It goes without saying that we leaders are only human, and we do sometimes mess up. I have occasionally lost my temper, or said something that I shouldn't have said, or acted in a way that asserted my authority when I didn't mean to. I'll get off a stressful phone call, for example, and then unintentionally snap at somebody.

But once again, this is a chance to take that setback and turn it into an opportunity. As quickly as I can—after I calm down and get my wits about me—I publicly go to the person I snapped at (and whoever else was there) to say, "I was out of line. I was stressed about a phone call, and I behaved inappropriately. You don't deserve that from me."

By doing this, I'm not only apologizing and taking responsibility; I'm showing them they are important enough to warrant a personal apology. I'm also demonstrating that I am human and make mistakes and that I have enough character to own up to them. If people understand that I am fallible—and if I am tolerant of their fallibility in return—it deepens our mutual trust.

Almost every single time there has been a problem in our company, it has to do with poor communication, and I would bet that many other leaders have a similar experience—particularly in an age when much of our communication is text and email that in many cases fail to fully express intention.

I recently went to a seminar led by Clark Brown, one of the trainers at the Cannon Financial Institute, an organization that provides advanced levels of training for financial advisors. I've learned a great deal about applied behavioral finance and communication from Mr. Brown.

At the seminar, Mr. Brown led us in a fascinating thought experiment. "Most advisors go into client meetings," he explained, "and say, 'Tell me how you feel about risk.' The client answers however they do: 'Oh, you know, I'm not too risky, but I'm not too conservative either, so I'd say I'm medium risk'—or whatever their answer is." The problem in communicating their answer is that everybody has a different idea of what risk means!

To explain the problem, Mr. Brown demonstrated with this exercise: he told us he was going to say a word, and he wanted us to share with him the first visualization that popped into our heads. The word he said was *horse*.

In my mind, I pictured a stallion, reddish brown, galloping through a field with black mane flying. I assumed (part of the problem!) that most other people probably pictured something similar—maybe a different color, maybe a different setting, but surely some kind of galloping horse.

Boy, was I wrong. In this class of about thirty people, some people did indeed picture a horse—but they pictured a horse plowing a field, a Kentucky Derby horse, or a cowboy on a bucking bronco. Others didn't picture an animal at all. "I was just thinking about shooting some hoops with my son the other day," the guy behind me said, "so I pictured the basketball game 'Horse.'"

"I'm just getting over being sick," another person chimed in, "so I thought of having a sore throat and being hoarse."

There were thirty different people in that classroom, and there were thirty entirely different images of *horse* (or *hoarse*, as the case may be). It all depends on your background, your history, your personal experiences, and even where you are specifically on that day, that hour, that minute. My picture of a horse was influenced by a painting of a horse that I have in my dining room. Nobody else would have that picture of a horse—that image is unique to my experience.

The same is true in many areas of life, including your individual picture of the word *risk*. I can't rely on my own interpretation to understand what *you* mean by "risk." I have to probe deeper. I have to follow up and say, "Tell me more about that. How do you feel when you lose money?" Or, "What's your biggest fear about losing money?" There are countless ways I can take the conversation deeper, but I can't just stop at that first question, because there are too many ways to interpret the answer.

In today's fast-paced world, we often move so quickly that we don't stop to understand that we are interpreting people's answers through our own filter. As a result, we often don't bother to ask more probing questions, to find out if the horse they're talking about is the one we're picturing in our mind.

If communication is the primary currency of the workplace, we must be better communicators by holding ourselves accountable for our words and actions. It isn't just the words; it's the meaning behind them. It's *how* we speak to the people we work with—when and why. We can be aware of the weight our words carry from our position in the company. We must take the time to really understand what the other person means, to dig deeper, to slow down and actually hear each other. At the end of the day, each of us is a person, and the most important part of being a person, in the workplace as in life, is building relationships with other people.

PART THREE

Relationship 301: A Graduate Course in Relationships

CHAPTER 11

Get Personal

People don't leave jobs; people leave people.

—WADE BREITZKE

Connecting is a basic human need. When you're traveling and you run into somebody who lives in your hometown, probably one of the first things you ask is, "What neighborhood do you live in?" We do this because we are always searching for common ground, for something that connects us. "Oh, I know that neighborhood!" we say. "Have you eaten at this restaurant?" Even if it's something as small as a restaurant we've both visited, we relish finding those personal connections. We are always looking for the threads that tie us together.

A friend of mine from Chicago was in Paris riding the subway. All around him, everybody was speaking in French. Then, somewhere near him, he heard somebody speaking English. Not only was he speaking in English—he was talking about the Chicago Cubs! Without hesitating, my friend turned around and said, "Hey, I heard you talking about the Cubs. I'm a Cubs fan too!" Even though they were total strangers, the desire to connect prompted him to grab onto that shared experience and start a deeper conversation.

This desire for connection is hardwired into our DNA. In prehistoric days, we learned that if we created tribes that had a common goal—to find food or to protect the village from danger—we learned to trust that we would work together as a group. This is what helped our species survive.

This instinct has stayed with us but now shows up in more subtle ways. The more commonality we can establish with other people, the more trust we can establish—and the more trust we can establish, the safer we feel. In today's world and in the workplace, that perceived safety leads to greater innovation and productivity, because you have a safety net of people to whom you are connected. You also know that you have a safe space to try out new ideas.

Connecting is essential to human beings. It's like the need to drink water, or eat, or go to the bathroom. It doesn't disappear just because you're in the office. Just as you can't ask people to go for eight hours without eating or using the bathroom, you shouldn't ask people to go eight hours without the same human connection they have outside work. And you can only really become deeply connected if you are willing to get personal.

We don't intentionally miss out on making personal connections in the workplace. In many cases it's simply because the appropriate and healthy environment has not been made available—it's just not part of the workplace culture. If you've been trained and brought up in a certain environment, if everybody around you is doing things a certain way, you're going to operate the same way—even if it's not your nature.

Many employers train people to keep their personal lives out of the workplace. As a result, sometimes it takes some significant changes to get people to open up. People believe they need to toe the line, to just do their job and not make waves, to not speak up about what they are passionate about, what their goals and dreams are. So sometimes you can't just ask a question and get a real answer. You have to keep asking and not accept the first superficial answer that someone gives.

To do this takes time, intentionality, and accountability. We're all so busy. We move so fast. We need to slow down and start to hold ourselves and each other accountable for better, more real answers. If someone asks you, "How have you been?" we usually get social colloquialisms—answers like, "Fine." "Busy." "I'm good; how are you?" We're becoming more and more desensitized to the questions. When you ask me how I'm doing and you let me get away with, "Fine, busy," and nothing else happens, you're helping me create a habit of giving automatic and superficial answers. There's a whole list of questions and answers that have become part of a script we follow and that don't actually carry any meaning—and are certainly not very personal.

We need to break away from the script. One of the ways we can do that—with our clients, our colleagues, everybody in our lives—is to hold ourselves and each other accountable for insincere questions and answers. We can press a little deeper. When someone answers, "Busy," ask, "Busy doing what? What have you been working on? Tell me about it."

We had an all-company meeting recently where I demonstrated this. I got up in front of the group, and said, "Okay, let me take a survey here. Hey, Jen, how's it going?"

"Fine," Jen said.

"Hey, John, how are you?"

"Busy," John said.

I couldn't have gotten more perfect responses to prove my point. I said, "Listen, we have to hold ourselves accountable. If we care about each other in this company, we can't let people get away with these polite, superficial responses all the time."

Of course, practically speaking, we can't do this all the time with every person we see. But we have to be aware of it so that we aren't constantly desensitizing each other to the same questions and answers. If you're not willing to probe and go deeper, if you don't want a real answer, don't ask the question. It's insincere.

Often, we may think we're having sincere, deeper conversations, but we are still just sitting on the surface. We may feel like we're giving or getting deeper answers when we start to share facts. But as we've discussed, just knowing the facts about someone isn't really knowing that person. The facts are important, but they don't get to the deeper, more personal knowledge it takes to develop meaningful relationships. By just asking that one-level-deeper question, I've changed the dynamic of the relationship. I've shown that I'm interested and that I care.

What many people don't realize is that even our stock "caring" answers can shut down the personal connection instead of opening it up. Perhaps the best example of this is the phrase *I understand*. That may feel empathetic, but it's actually just another one of those colloquial, polite, superficial responses. It's become so automatic that we don't realize the effect it has. What "I understand" really does is shut down the conversation. It says, "You don't need to tell me anymore, because I understand already." I've terminated the conversation. If you say, "My kids are a nightmare," and I say, "I understand," I don't really understand. I'm trying to bridge the gap, but I'm discounting what you're going through.

In a recent edition of his newsletter for people in the financial services industry, Nick Murray wrote that if people call you and say they're worried about the stock market, the worst thing you can possibly say is, "I understand." Because you can't. You can understand *your* version of what they're going through, but you can't understand *their* version unless you get more information.

Instead of saying, "I understand," take that opportunity to ask a deeper-level question. When someone says they're worried about the market, you can say, for instance, "How do you feel about it?"

"I feel scared about my investments."

"Okay, what is it that scares you the most about them?"

Soon, you'll get to the real heart of the matter, to a deeper conversation, to a better understanding of what the person is dealing with and looking for. Moreover, when people are scared, they tend to use the instinctual part of the brain, the amygdala, that contains the fight-or-flight response. When I start asking questions, when I start digging for deeper and more complex answers, I pull that person out of his or her instinctual brain and back to the cerebral cortex, where logical thought occurs, and the fear generally subsides.

When you start having those deeper conversations—with clients, with colleagues—you start to care, and people know it. Caring is born the moment I invite you to share something that is not your stock answer. Intimacy is created both ways. If I start asking more questions, start delving deeper, then I start to care—and you can tell that I care. When you can tell that I care, you're not going to give me a hollow response.

I'm a student of nonverbal communication. Depending on your source, it has been said that less than 20 percent of communication is actually the words you use. I've found that once I get past that superficial first-level question, and then past the second level and on to the third question that's going a little deeper, people's body language changes. They lean into you. They turn their shoulders to face you. Their body language indicates that they're ready to share. And then you can feel the physical release that accompanies the personal information—and you know you've reached that deeper level.

The responsibility for these deeper interchanges falls on both sides. If you're starting the conversation, don't let the other person get away with canned answers. But if someone asks you an automatic question, don't let them get away with that either. Provide a thoughtful response, which will in turn elicit a deeper response from them. You can unwrap each other.

If I start opening up, that will make it much easier for you to open up in response. If I say, "Let me tell you about my day—here's what happened," that opens the door for you to say, "I had an experience like that last week; let me tell you about it." Then the conversation becomes a memorable interchange that deepens the relationship.

This is true for every individual, but as a leader, it is up to you to set the tone in the workplace. If that tone is one of openness, intimacy, and vulnerability, you'll get that same warmth back from your team, and those meaningful relationships will be nurtured. Part of being a leader is being the first one to do it—the one to open the door.

The best way to invite and create intimacy is by being willing to be vulnerable first. That speeds up the process dramatically. If I'm the first one to share a meaningful moment about myself, if I'm the first one to tell you about a mistake I made or share a special thought, then you will be much more open to sharing in return.

At Lakeside, when people come into the office on Monday,

they are usually talking about and sharing what they did over the weekend, what's going on in their lives—the good, the bad, the ugly. This happens because we've created an environment in our workplace that encourages and cultivates that kind of communication. And that starts with the leader. If I am willing to chime in, to talk about my weekend, to say that I did something dumb or something funny, then other people will chime in too. Soon everybody joins the conversation, and we're all having fun. If I come in, say, "Good morning," and walk straight to my office, I'm not creating a warm environment. It's a very different message. It's not approachable.

I'm also open to admitting when I have a problem. I might say, "I don't know if this ever happens to you, but this happened to me the other day, and I don't know what to do with it. What do you think?" Someone with a perceived position of authority coming to someone at a lower-level position and saying, "Listen, I've got a problem, and I could use some help. Will you help me?" really demonstrates that I trust and value that person. One of the biggest compliments you can pay somebody is to ask for their advice. The implied trust and respect that go into asking for someone's advice speak volumes.

Now I want to be clear about something: getting personal doesn't mean having to answer questions you don't want to answer. It's about creating an environment where you can share as much as you want, but you don't feel uncomfortable and compelled to share when you don't want to.

Moreover, personal doesn't always mean problematic. It doesn't always mean sharing problems or painful things. At our last Christmas party, an advisor who'd been working for us for several years went up while the band was on a break, picked up a guitar, and started playing. I had no idea that he was a musician, and I got really excited—because I'm a musician too! Soon we ended up in a great deep, personal conversation about why we are so passionate about music. That is just as personal and intimate as any personal problem I might share. In fact, getting personal over something fun and positive is a great way to start developing those deeper relationships

Of course, developing relationships and maintaining connections aren't easy tasks. They take work. You have to be very intentional about it. There are realistic limitations on how many people we can really put in the work and be friends with.

Keith Ferrazzi points out that this is where technology can help us. Some argue that technology is making us more isolated. That's true in some ways, but it can also be used to help us connect and bring us even closer.

You can use technology, Ferrazzi says, to keep yourself organized. Let's say I'm working on developing my relationship with you. I can use my digital calendar to schedule a recurring monthly or quarterly action such as, "Touch base with so-and-so." That may just be me giving you a call and saying, "Hey, what's going on?" But it helps me remember, in the midst of my busy schedule, to stay in touch and keep fostering that connection. And of course, I use my calendar to keep track of people's birthdays, so I can make my infamous birthday phone calls!

I think there can be a combination, a middle ground, that leverages both the technology of social media and real-life interactions to benefit human relationships across the board.

Social media also plays a huge role in how we connect with each other. I think there is some validity to the argument some make that social media is compromising people's ability to interact in real life. But I don't think it's an either/or situation. I think it can be an "and." I think there can be a combination, a middle ground, that leverages both the technology of social media and real-life interactions to benefit human relationships across the board.

Most people connect with their coworkers on social media, and once you do that, you've already started to connect with them on a personal level. In some ways, I think social media can even lead to more directed and targeted conversations, if not more meaningful ones. If you post something and your colleague sees it, instead of asking, "How did your weekend go?" she can ask specifically about whatever you posted.

Of course, to have intimate communication on a day-to-day basis doesn't require social media. Social media is a tool that many people—especially millennials—use to facilitate deeper conversation, connection, and intimacy, but it's not a prerequisite for having those relationships. You can have those relationships if you just engage in a deeper level of communication when you're face to face.

It's easier to foster relationships with people you see every day. But there are some people who I see only at a conference once a year, or if we happen to be in the same city at the same time. This is where I leverage technology to help grow relationships. I use my Outlook calendar, for example, to keep my network organized. When I'm visiting a city, I used LinkedIn to see which of my contacts live there.

My partner, Tim Rice, does this brilliantly. I have never met somebody so organized around managing his calendar efficiently *and* working on relationships. He was in New York recently for a meeting, and he spent the whole week prior making phone calls to everybody he knew in New York. He was going to be there for only a day and a half, but he wanted to connect with as many people as possible. Even though many of the people weren't available, it still strengthened the relationship, because Tim took the time to call and try to make plans—the effort itself is part of the connection.

Ferrazzi also writes that preparation is key when starting and building relationships. In fact, if I had not been prepared, I would never have met Don Connelly! Don is a legend in the financial services industry for his motivational speeches and sales training.[4] he was the speaker at a conference I was attending, so I started doing a little homework. As I started to read about him, I became more and more interested in his work. So I dug a little deeper and found that he lives in Sarasota, Florida, and that he plays golf. I also play golf, and, at the time, I had a place in Fort Myers, just half an hour away from Sarasota. We actually had a lot more in common, but I had enough background to start a conversation.

I went to the conference, and sure enough, he gave an amazing speech. Right as he was wrapping up, I left my seat and walked over to where I knew he was going to exit the stage. When he left the stage, I stuck my hand out and said, "Hey, Don. My name's Mark Chamberlain. I'm an advisor in the Chicago area. I really enjoyed your speech. I'd love to see if I can get our company to book you as a speaker at one of our events. Do you have a card? Also, I noticed that you live in Sarasota; I have a place in Fort Myers myself. Tell me, have you ever golfed at …" And within thirty seconds, we had made the connection. Thirty seconds, and we've kept in touch ever since—going on nine years now. None of that would have happened if I hadn't been prepared.

Intentionality and preparation aren't just important for starting a new relationship or for people you see only a few times a year. You also need to be intentional about fostering a real, personal connection with the people you see every day. One of the ways I try to do this

---

4   You can learn more about Don and his work at www.donconnelly247.com.

is by having a one-on-one lunch with every employee at least once or twice a year. Fortunately, with about forty employees, Lakeside is the right size to make this easy to schedule. Depending on the size of your organization, this might not be possible, but you can still strive for something along these lines, such as encouraging supervisors to have one-on-one lunches with the people who report to them.

At these lunches, I try not to talk specifically about business—with the exception of asking about where they want to be in their career in five years, as we talked about earlier. I mostly focus on them as a person. I try to do my homework before these lunches so I can ask specific meaningful questions about their family, their interests, and the things they care about.

In these conversations, I want to show the person that I am genuinely interested in and care about him or her. I also let employees know immediately that I don't mind if our lunch goes over an hour. This time is just as important to me as the rest of my job. Getting to know what's going on in their lives, hearing their thoughts, having a meaningful conversation—all that is more important than getting back to the office.

If I make a point of having lunch with you one on one, it shows that I consider you just as important as I am. It breaks down the barrier between us and creates a greater sense of equality. I try to emphasize this by letting them know that they are just as much in control of the interaction as I am. When I make these lunch plans, I'll always ask them where they want to eat. "Oh, I don't care," the person will often say. "It's up to you."

"No," I tell them. "It's not up to me. This lunch is about you. Where do you want to have lunch? Do you want me to cook for you? Do you want sushi, Indian, Mexican? Whatever you like, I'm there!" This sets the stage for the conversation that happens during lunch, because it gives them control—and thereby makes the whole encounter more welcoming and approachable.

Approachable has become one of my favorite words. If you can make both the client experience and colleague interaction approachable, a lot of good things happen. And fostering approachability extends beyond person-to-person interactions as well—it is also part of creating an environment.

CHAPTER 12

It's Not an Office— It's an Environment

We strive to make our workplace the
ultimate talent destination.

—MARK W. CHAMBERLAIN

The physical environment of a workplace can have a huge effect on everything we've been discussing in the previous chapters. If the relationship between employer and employee can evolve, so should the physical workspace. It's hard to change workplace culture if the physical space still adheres to old ways of working. Taking down the cultural walls between people is difficult if the physical walls still stand, separating everyone—and preventing them from enjoying coming to work.

Nobody wants to leave their house and spend their day in a

depressing environment, one that is neither exciting nor motivational. So when Lakeside moved to our current space, we asked, "What makes home so appealing? What things at home do I miss when I'm at work?" And we started creating our physical space based on that question.

When you walk into the offices at Lakeside, the first thing you see after you pass the reception desk is a big light-filled space with tables and a full open state-of-the-art kitchen. This space was deliberately designed from scratch, inspired by our experience in our first office space.

Lakeside's first office was in a rehabbed house that I enlarged three times, until we eventually ran out of land. We had thirty-five people working there and one unisex bathroom—that gives you an idea of what kind of space it was!

In what used to be the kitchen of the house, we had a small office kitchen with a table. During lunchtime, everyone in the office would try to squeeze into the kitchen, wheeling in extra chairs and sitting two deep around the table. And that was just for ordinary, everyday lunches. You can imagine how packed it got every time someone had a birthday, or we had an office potluck, or there was any other kind of special occasion. Everybody wanted to socialize in the kitchen.

When it became clear that we could no longer fit into the rehabbed house, we started searching for a bigger office, and we found the building we occupy now. The building had been built in 2008, right before the recession. The bottom floor was leased out the day it was built, but thanks to the real estate market crash, the top floor had remained vacant.

We felt we only needed nine or ten thousand square feet, but we were convinced by the owner to take more or less the whole top floor—about fifteen thousand square feet. The owner then gave us a pile of money to build it out any way we wanted.

"Anything we want, eh?" I thought—and the first thing I asked our architect to design was a kitchen.

The architect designed a pretty standard office kitchen—a tight enclosed space with a fridge, a microwave, a sink, and room for a table and some chairs.

"No, no," I said. "That's not what I mean. We want a *real* kitchen."

If you are entertaining people at your house, it's universally true that no matter where you set up the snacks and beverages, everybody inevitably ends up in the kitchen. No matter the layout, the kitchen is always the social hub of a house. Recognizing that as the natural human inclination, why wouldn't you try to re-create it in the workplace? In order for a workspace to feel more personal, comfortable, and homelike, a centralized, accessible kitchen is essential.

Once we had decided to design this kitchen space, we had to decide what we wanted it to look like. We knew we didn't want it to look like a classic Wall Street office space, with dark leather chairs and walnut walls. We wanted it to feel friendly, open, approachable—a space for socialization and collaboration.

We knew we wanted to use the kitchen as a space for events, such as client events, potlucks, or employee birthdays. We had no idea it would be used consistently for day-to-day dining. For the first couple of weeks in the new space, everybody was cramming into the back room to have lunch. Then people started migrating out into the front kitchen area. After all, we had this big, beautiful space; naturally, people wanted to eat there!

As we saw this migration happen, we asked, "Why not push this a little further?" We started buying a little food to keep in the fridge—nothing crazy, just fresh fruit and some staples. Soon people weren't just eating in the kitchen area; they were cooking there too. In fact, it's become a regular part of Lakeside life. Let me tell you— we throw quite a potluck!

Food is a universal socializing force. All over the world, in every culture, people come together over food. By bringing that force into the workplace culture, you can use food as a way to grow and strengthen those all-important personal connections.

There is almost nothing more intimate than cooking for someone. I've started using it as a way to build personal relationships more quickly. In the process, I discovered that it's a great professional development tool as well. If I take you out to breakfast and pick up the tab, that's a nice gesture. If I cook you breakfast myself, I've taken a risk. You might not like what I cook. I could mess it up. I've made myself vulnerable, and that vulnerability creates an automatic level of trust. When that level of trust is established, it is easier for the other person to open up and be vulnerable in return—which creates a stronger advisor-client relationship.

Personal finance is incredibly intimate, and most clients have aspects of their financial lives they are embarrassed to share. They keep certain things compartmentalized and are unsure about revealing them. If I can unlock those compartments by encouraging the client to be open and vulnerable with me, I become a better advisor. Cooking breakfast for someone, I've discovered, is an amazing first step in helping that happen. I encourage everybody who works here to cook breakfast or lunch for people, even if they don't consider themselves cooks. In fact, I tell them, it just makes them more vulnerable, which is better.

The kitchen came about through a lot of intention and a bit of luck—the lucky opportunity of having a blank canvas on which to implement our design. But without the intention, I guarantee you won't find the luck. If you're creative and open to opportunity, good things will happen around you—including things you never expected.

At Lakeside, the energy of the kitchen started to influence our thinking about other spaces in the office, and the environment started to build on itself. Employees felt the energy, too, and started coming up with ideas of their own. One day, someone came in and said, "I've got an extra beanbag toss at home; why don't we put that in the empty space at the back of the office?" Now we have a beanbag toss. Someone else said, "My partner's an artist; why don't we have a little gallery where we can display art?" Now we have an art gallery, complete with a couch from which to admire the paintings. Sometimes we bring clients there for meetings, because it is such a warm, creative environment.

Very quickly, the focus shifted from how my partner and I wanted the space to look and feel to how everybody else in the company wanted it to look and feel. That, in turn, gave our staff a great sense of ownership over the space. We gave them the permission to generate ideas, and they ran with it, creating a work environment they truly enjoy.

That permission was easy to grant. We simply had to say, "This is where you work, and we want you to be comfortable and happy while you work. What do we need to do to create that space?" That question bridged the gap and opened the conversation—and people responded. Instead of the leadership team providing all the answers, the team is engaged in the process, the feedback, and the workspace.

This kind of collaboration is something we wanted to foster throughout the workplace. Therefore, our whole office is designed to feel open and to foster open communication and collaboration. At a typical investment office, each advisor has his or her own book of accounts and works for individual commissions. If you have twenty advisors, it's akin to having twenty separate businesses all operating under one roof. At Lakeside, everybody is on salary. Nobody's on commission. Instead of having separate offices out of which each advisor runs his or her own little business, our office is open and collaborative. It's communal, and everyone works toward a common purpose.

Of course, this can create some challenges. Sometimes it can get noisy. Sometimes people need a quiet space to concentrate on a difficult task or a private space in which to have a confidential conversation or phone call. To account for these needs, we created designated quiet and private spaces throughout the office.

We're not the only company making these kinds of adjustments. We have a client in Michigan City that occupies an older building. Over the years, the company has put on around twenty-four additions to that building. Now it's like a labyrinth. You need a map to get from the marketing department to the accounting department—even if you work there. Nobody's connected with anybody else.

The client decided to spend a significant amount of money to rehab and remodel the space, creating a better flow from one area to the next, moving departments around so they can connect with each other more easily. The company has a decent workplace culture, so the HR director was surprised and frustrated by the vehement pushback he got from employees when this remodel was announced. The people who have worked there for forty years didn't want anything to change.

This is not an isolated phenomenon. In their book, *Change Your Space, Change Your Culture*, Rex Miller, Mabel Casey, and Mark Konchar write that overcoming resistance to change is a huge part of reinventing a company culture. In fact, a whole line of consultants exists who focus specifically on change culture—not just on the physical changes but on overcoming resistance to change.

When we created our open plan, we got some pushback—and we still do. Some people aren't crazy about sharing a big open space with all their colleagues. My view is that if you're working here, you are part of a community. By all sharing the same space, we encourage the community environment that is core to the Lakeside ethos.

Of course, creating a community and a community environment doesn't happen simply by altering the physical surroundings. You can build the physical space, but if it's not accompanied by the right attitude, then the space won't be used in the way you intend.

The workplace is not simply a bunch of separate individuals who happen to be in the same place working for the same company. It's a community. Communities support each other, care about each other, and do things for the good of the communal whole. You can tell when a neighborhood has a strong community—when residents care about the communal whole. People know their neighbors. There are neighborhood block parties. The parks are well kept because everybody cares about their shared environment.

The same can be true at work. If you create a true community, everybody will care about the workplace and about each other. They will be eager to contribute because they are concerned with the collective well-being of the community.

Part of the responsibility of living in a community is being aware of those around you. With an open floor plan, the community becomes self-policing. Because people care about the company, each other, and the community, nobody wants to be the person who's not pulling his or her weight. Everybody wants to be positively contributing and wants to be seen positively contributing, because everybody cares.

Good community self-policing isn't about shaming people or calling people out. It's about helping the community as a whole. If a neighbor is letting his or her yard become overgrown, and it is tarnishing the beauty of the block or even becoming dangerous, a strong community will rally not to shame that neighbor but to encourage and perhaps help the neighbor clean up the yard, so the whole community benefits.

If you have a good tribe, the tribe encourages positive behavior much more than discipline does. Dave Logan, John King, and Halee Fischer-Wright discuss this in their book, *Tribal Leadership*. In a level-four tribe, there is tribal pride, an attitude of "we're great" as opposed to "I'm great." If you hire people into a level-four tribe who previously worked for a level-two or level-three tribe, your tribe will improve their behavior. It happens very organically. New hires will come from a dysfunctional company, and once they are embedded in the new more functional tribe, their behavior will almost inevitably change to match that of their colleagues.

When the people around us truly care and are doing outstanding work, we naturally want to rise to meet that standard. We want to be part of that community of excellence. We don't want to be the weakest link in a strong community. The people in the community who don't care about the work, the company, or the community will eventually be weeded out. The community both applies pressure to step up and encourages, helps, and inspires people to step up.

The important fact is that impetus for stepping up comes from the community, not from a supervisor telling you what to do. If you are really a part of the community, a part of the tribe, if you care about the people in the village and the communal welfare of the village, you're going to care a lot more about keeping it safe through the night. It almost doesn't matter whether the leader instructed you to guard the village; you're doing it for the sake of the community.

Of course, as a leader, it is essential to be a fully integrated part of the community. When we were much smaller, one of our standard job interview questions was, "Are you willing to pitch in wherever you can around here? Because we don't have a lot of people." Everybody had to do their part—even when it came to maintenance tasks like taking out the trash.

That everybody-pitch-in ethic persists. Even today, after we have an event or after-lunch hour, I tie up garbage bags behind the counter, right alongside everybody else. When I demonstrate that it's not beneath me to take out the garbage, I reinforce that we are all on equal footing, and that inspires everybody to pitch in.

I always try to stand shoulder to shoulder with the rest of the company. Our company organizes group volunteering events for not-for-profit organizations. One of the organizations we work with regularly is Rebuilding Together, which improves housing for elderly and low-income residents. A group of Lakeside employees, along with their spouses and kids, will go out to a job site to put in new carpeting, paint the walls, or otherwise fix up homes.

I always participate in these events. Once, I was pulling the carpeting off the floor so we could replace it. One of my millennial employees had brought his parents along to volunteer. I was filthy and sweaty, down on my hands and knees, work gloves on my hands, and Corey said, "Hey, Mark, I want you to meet my parents!" I stood up, took off my glove, and shook hands with his mom and dad. And Corey said, with a pride in his voice that I'll never forget, "This is Mark. He's our CEO." He wanted his parents to know that the CEO of the company he worked for was down on his hands and knees ripping up carpet with everybody else. It was part of why he liked working for us. He was proud of the environment our company creates: a community where we are all in it together.

When the leader is truly a part of the tribe, the tribe takes care of the leader. In the military at mealtimes, the lowest-ranking soldiers eat first, and the general eats last. The general has the wisdom to know that without the people on the front line, he has nothing. Despite being at the end of the food line, no general has ever gone hungry. The soldiers in the line understand that the general needs to be well nourished and on his toes to keep them out of harm's way. And the general trusts that his troops will ensure there is still food left for him when he gets there.

Planning activities in which everyone can participate can greatly strengthen the community of the workplace. At Lakeside, we have potlucks, holiday events, and volunteer projects. We also have Flat Lou—our version of the Flat Stanley initiative for second or third graders. Flat Stanley is a cartoon character that kids cut out and color, then send through the mail to family members or friends. The family members and friends then take pictures of Flat Stanley doing different fun things in different locations and send those back to the kids. Then the kids write an adventure story about where Flat Stanley has been.

We took that concept and created our own character named Flat Lou after our office dog. Everyone in the company has a Flat Lou; the challenge is to photograph Flat Lou wherever you go.

We get pictures from all over the country. I was in Las Vegas recently and went to a bar that seemed right out of a mob movie. A lounge singer at the bar, Kevin D., looked straight out of central casting, gold chains and all. Of course, I said, "Hey, Kevin, I want to take a picture with you and Flat Lou!" We took a picture, and now part of Flat Lou's adventure is going to a mob bar in Vegas!

All the pictures get sent to Jen, our corporate communications manager, who prints and adds them to a bulletin board in the office on which we track Flat Lou's journey. Everybody wants to have their Flat Lou picture up on the board. People are on a mission to take the most creative picture of Flat Lou! Jen also posts the pictures on our social media accounts and sends out a weekly email, so everybody can keep up on Flat Lou's adventures.

The Flat Lou exercise, as silly as it seems, allows everyone in the company to connect on a personal level, breaking down the wall between workplace and personal life. Thanks to Flat Lou, people are excited to share what they did over the weekend or on vacation. Flat Lou also allows our offices in other places to be a part of the bigger Lakeside community. People in our Wisconsin office can send in Flat Lou pictures, and they are posted on the billboard and on our Facebook page alongside those from the main Chesterton office. Flat Lou creates a bridge between offices and between colleagues, creating a more seamless integration between work life and personal life.

A true community is a group of people who are there for you when you need help, including in your personal life. Just recently, I was going out of town, as was my daughter, and we needed somewhere for my dog, Lou, to stay while we were away. I hardly had to ask before someone in the office offered to take him for those four days. Someone else was going out of town and needed someone to drop off and pick up her cat from where he was being boarded—and once again, a colleague stepped right up.

Speaking of dogs, what are the two things people miss the most when they're at work? Their kids and their pets. How do we solve that? For pets, it's easy: our office dog, Lou, comes in every day. Dogs feel like home. They bring comfort and coziness—and, of course, fun!

We also encourage people to bring their families into the office.

Many of our employees have children, so we also make sure to create a welcoming environment for kids. If daddy's off one day, and he wants to bring the kids in, go for it! We have dozens of people who want to hold babies. We also intentionally create kid-centered events. Santa visited the office last Christmas, and we had almost thirty kids here! We baked and decorated Christmas cookies, and everyone had a wonderful time.

> If I'm going to integrate my personal life into my work life, and part of my personal life is having fun, shouldn't work have a fun component to it as well? Shouldn't it be okay to not take ourselves too seriously? We shouldn't have to lose our playfulness just because we're adults.

If I'm going to integrate my personal life into my work life, and part of my personal life is having fun, shouldn't work have a fun component to it as well? Shouldn't it be okay to not take ourselves too seriously? We shouldn't have to lose our playfulness just because we're adults.

At Lakeside, fun is an integral part of the work environment—and I always try to be a ringleader for that fun. Before our last company meeting, our head of corporate communications sent out a survey with questions such as, "Whose desk are you most likely to lose your pen on?" and other superlatives. Everyone voted, and at the company meeting, we awarded the winners. One of the questions was, "Who has the most fun in the office?" Somebody else won that, and I have never been more upset to lose a prize!

The ability to participate in or even instigate fun in the workplace is part of being a good leader. As I've said, one of my favorite words is *approachability*. Sometimes, titles like CEO can make people see you as unapproachable. If you combine that with behavior that could be read as unapproachable, you can become impenetrable. No matter the size of the company, it is important for the CEO to be physically approachable but also personally and emotionally approachable.

That's why I like to break out the Nerf darts.

"Nerf darts?" you might be thinking. "This guy is crazy!"

Well, maybe so—but it is also endless fun. One of my favorite pranks is the one I pull on new employees. While they're sitting at their desk working on their computer, I sneak up behind them with my Nerf gun and shoot a dart right by their ear so it sticks on their computer screen. It scares the hell out of them—and then we all share a good laugh. This simple prank creates a sense of fun and camaraderie and lets new people know right away that we don't take ourselves too seriously.

I also have a favorite April Fools' Day trick to play on new people. I give the number of a local zoo to the new employee and say, "Hey, would you call this number and ask for Mr. Bear, and tell him that I'd like to make an appointment with him for such and such?" They do as I ask, call the zoo, and ask for Mr. Bear. Everybody who's been in the office knows that this is my favorite joke, so when I pull it on someone, we all listen in on the call—and when the new employee realizes the joke, we once again all share a hearty laugh. I've done this so many times that the zoo employees have come to expect these calls. When someone calls asking for Mr. Bear, they immediately say, "You're from Lakeside, right?"

By having fun with my employees, I have a good time—and I create camaraderie with all the people in the company. If people are comfortable with me, if they feel like they can slug me on the shoulder, if they feel we can poke fun at each other, we create a more comfortable, productive, and fun environment for everyone. After all, who wants to be a parent, a security guard, and a boss all day, every day? Not me!

Moreover, these fun releases actually boost productivity. My career at the Chicago Board of Trade certainly did not prioritize relationships, but I did have a lot of fun. In between the bouts of dog-eat-dog intensity, we'd sit around and yuck it up with the best of them. An important part of our environment was the ability to blow off steam between all the stress.

All work can be stressful. When you work from home, you can take a break, get up and stretch, turn on the TV for a minute, or go outside to give your brain a break and get back on track. Traditional offices, both in design and mood, aren't conducive to that kind of flexibility. However, we can create an environment that allows for the same releases I had as a trader—while still maintaining productivity.

Employers are finally starting to accept the idea that humans aren't robots. Unlike robots, humans need to take brief mental or physical breaks from work to recharge. Being able to release some of the pressure of day-to-day work adds immensely to the quality of life in the workplace—and if that results in an uptick in productivity, so much the better!

The idea of bringing some zany fun into the workplace is not mine alone. At Zappos, Tony Hsieh, the CEO, has instituted ten core values by which Zappos employees live and work—values he writes about in his book, *Delivering Happiness*. Number three on the list is "create fun and a little weirdness."

This value is immediately apparent when you tour Zappos' Las Vegas headquarters. Zappos is very open to having visitors tour the building. They want you, as a consumer, to feel connected to the company. Anybody who works at Zappos can lead a tour, which means the tours are led by members of the Zappos community. As a result, everyone on the tour feels welcomed by part of the family.

On the tour, visitors experience the personality of the company. They witness the happiness and enjoyment apparent among the staff, which demonstrates the higher standard to which a business can be held. That standard, that work environment, is one consumers want to propagate and support.

The Zappos employees get as much out of the tour experience as the visitors do. They feel pride in their office as they show it off on the tour—and they have fun while they do. In fact, if you come for a visit wearing a tie, a Zappos team member will get a big pair of scissors, cut your tie in half, and then hang it up on the wall. You won't be alone—there are hundreds of ties up on that wall!

I've tried to mimic elements of the Zappos attitude in our office at Lakeside. I encourage all of our staff to give tours, to explain all the cool and different aspects of our office, and to take pride in the environment we've created. I love eavesdropping, hearing how each person tells the story of Lakeside and how they personally connect to working here.

My friends and fellow CEOs laugh at many of the choices we make about our environment. They don't understand why we spend money on non-work-specific amenities. The kitchen gets a lot of raised eyebrows when people visit our office for the first time. One of my friends could not believe that we provide food for people. "It's not much; it's just some staples," I tried to explain. "It only adds up to around $500 a month." To him, that was absurd. To me, the connections, community, and energy we get in return are more than worth it.

These elements all make the workplace more enjoyable for the employees—but they make it more enjoyable for me too. I can't wait to come to work because I know others can't wait to come to work. With all the incredible energy in the office, I can't bear the thought of my colleagues being at work without me. It feels like not getting invited to a party.

I'm not the only one who thinks this way. If you ask anybody in the office what our Friday mantra is, they'll tell you, "Only two more days until Monday!" With that level of excitement, going to work is not a chore or an obligation. We *want* to go to work. We think, "I get to go to work, and I can't wait."

Although some may question our practices, I know that my priorities are in the right place because Lakeside attracts people who share a similar belief system and mission. The only evidence I need to support our efforts to create a great workplace environment is the fact that I love coming to work—and everybody else at Lakeside loves coming to work too.

CHAPTER 13

Treat People the Right Way

If you want to go fast, go alone. If you
want to go far, go together.

—AFRICAN PROVERB

As the title of this book implies, you need to give people a reason for wanting to work for and with you. I am talking about engagement that goes beyond financially related motivation. Financially related rewards become commodities and are fairly limiting when you look closely at what moves people over an extended period of time.

This concept is particularly important for business owners and executives because they are moved by different stimuli. An owner or executive who benefits directly from profitability or the reward of things like ownership and stock options has a different stake in the game.

I know I am not alone in the experience that somehow stakeholders care *differently* than nonstakeholders. Notice I did not say care *more*—just differently. Once I understood this dynamic, I stopped being frustrated with it. I was able to slow down and say, "Okay, they (employees) are going to look at this differently than I do. They are going to need different things to move them than the things that move and inspire me in the workplace. So the question becomes, How can we bridge the gap in other ways?"

It starts with treating people the right way.

When we get lazy in our relationships, it can become very easy to see people as just the means to an end. This happens everywhere in life. It even happens in our personal relationships. At home, the courtship period can wear off, and we start thinking of our mates in terms of the function they play in our lives—contributing income, helping raise the kids, and so on. Over time, it can become easy to start taking them for granted—not maliciously, but out of routine.

This can be especially true in the workplace. It's easy, through daily routine, to say to someone, "I need you here because of what you can do, not because of who you are." Once you start doing that, it's hard to peel the label off. You start to think of that individual as a function rather than a person. You just think of them in terms of their job, in terms of what they produce. In turn, their response to being treated like the means to an end rather than a valuable and unique individual can begin to deteriorate behavior and engagement.

Treating people the right way means viewing them as people first—not as just a means to an end. You have to look beyond what you want to get *out of* them and care more about what you can add *to* them.

I've seen so many people in business treat their customers like royalty and then turn around and regard their colleagues as second-class citizens. I think that's a dangerous attitude—and a slippery slope. Another telling example is if I'm out to dinner with people and I see them treating the waitstaff with less consideration than they treat me. That will make me lose respect for them. There's no integrity in that kind of behavior, and it can be an indication of how they conduct themselves in other areas. Employees can sense it—and so can customers.

On the other hand, if you treat your work colleagues with equal dignity and respect as you would your biggest customer, you begin building leadership based on trust. That energy begins to seep into the customer experience, and they can sense the happiness and fulfillment that becomes part of the interaction. As a consumer, I'm inclined to patronize companies where the leaders act and treat their colleagues that way. I would much rather spend my money where employees are happy versus a business where they are miserable, because it changes *my* experience too.

For many consumers, it's becoming more important to consume products and services from organizations that they respect. Many people—particularly millennials—are paying more attention to the culture of the companies they buy from. People are naturally drawn to—and more likely to choose—companies that align with their values.

Any number of books and articles that discuss company culture and values note the connection between the vision and values of consumers and the companies that get their business in today's economy. Starbucks, Southwest Airlines, and Zappos are some of the many examples of companies today that connect with their customers beyond the actual products they sell. In most cases, the success of these companies in connecting with consumers in a deeper way is possible because of the interaction that happens between the frontline employee and the customer.

Arguably, this improved interaction between customer and employee can be attributed to some extent to the improved interaction between the employee and the employer. Energy, enthusiasm, and a smile beget energy, enthusiasm, and a smile!

When clients walk into the Lakeside space, they can immediately see and feel the energy of the office. They can tell that the people who work here love it, are happy and engaged, and care about the company and each other. The distinct energy of our office is so palpable that we actually have employees who were referred to us by clients!

One young man worked at a local bank, and two of my clients, as well as one of my employees, recommended him to us. "He's very sharp," they all said, "and he would fit right in with the Lakeside culture."

The fact that three people recommended this young man shows that our clients, as well as our employees, understand who we are and how we operate—otherwise, how could they have known that he'd fit right in? The people who knew this person cared about him as much as they did about us. They wouldn't have referred him to us if they thought it was a bad place for him to work or a poor choice for us to hire.

When you treat people the right way, you barely need recruiters or advertising. Your employees can't help but talk about how different the company they work for is. And when they meet someone who would be a good fit for our company, they usually try to recruit him or her for us!

The same is true of clients. If they identify the values and connect with the energy as soon as they come into the building—never mind throughout the rest of the business relationship—they are going to go out and do a commercial for me, which is much more effective than self-promotion.

Treating people right is also a very effective way to keep your people around. Every leader wants loyal employees. I certainly do, and I believe that Lakeside can be a lifelong workplace. The question is, How do you turn your staff into lifers?

Many companies promote the value of their benefits as a way to encourage loyalty. But the fact is, many of the kinds of benefits that were so exceptional back in the day are now fairly common and don't separate employers the way benefits used to. Saying, "We're so great, we offer this and this," is no longer enough to keep employees loyal. Instead, you must shift the focus to the employee. Now, instead of saying, "We're so awesome as an employer, so you should stick around," you say, "You're so awesome as an employee; we really appreciate you here; you are in indispensable part of this company and this community."

This can start as early as the hiring process. Obviously, the people being hired need us because they need a job. What we should make clearer as leaders is that we need them as much as they need us. "Our tribe needs you to be part of the tribe, part of this community. You're going to make this place better." Wouldn't that be a cool thing to hear when somebody makes you a job offer?

"I need you" is a vulnerable statement, especially if you're a big successful company. Sharing that vulnerability says to people, "I see you; I see your talent; I value you. You're going to make us better; we would not be as good without you." It lets them know that they are indispensable and appreciated—which will make them more inclined to want to stick around.

It's the difference between pushing and pulling. I can't push you to feel something. But if I do the right things, I can pull you in. It's my responsibility to create the environment that pulls you in.

There is a famous fable by Aesop that sums up this point nicely:

"The Wind and the Sun were disputing which was the stronger. Suddenly they saw a traveler coming down the road, and the Sun said: 'I see a way to decide our dispute. Whichever of us can cause that traveler to take off his cloak shall be regarded as the stronger. You begin.' So the Sun retired behind a cloud, and the Wind began to blow as hard as it could upon the traveler. But the harder he blew the more closely did the traveler wrap his cloak 'round him, till at last the Wind had to give up in despair. Then the Sun came out and shone in all his glory upon the traveler, who soon found it too hot to walk with his cloak on."[5]

I can't push people to want to work for me. But I *can* pull in them by creating a good, caring, and empowering environment. I can pull them in by treating them right. If I do that, not only will they want to work for me—they won't want to leave.

Since I started our business, the best compliment I've ever received was from an employee. I was looking for some honest feedback about my leadership, and I asked her what she liked best about working for me. Her answer: "Your flexibility."

This particular employee was one of our earliest hires, and she'd been with us for more than a decade. She loved working at Lakeside, but her kids were understandably her priority. She wanted to be there when the kids got off the bus; she wanted to be able to see her kids in the school play. So back when her kids were young, she asked if she could work for us part time. Because of that, she's been able to raise her kids from grade school to college on her own terms, knowing that we supported her in that choice. By doing that, we allowed her

---

5   Aesop, "The Wind and the Sun," in *Harvard Classics, Vol. 17, Part 1* (New York: P. F. Collier & Son, 1909–14), https://www.bartleby.com/17/1/60.html.

to be her best self, both at work and at home.

Why wouldn't you want your team to be their best selves in all areas of their lives? Why wouldn't you want them to be happy and fulfilled, at work and at home? Why would you want them to have a growing resentment toward work, because it is taking them away from the important things in their personal lives?

Of course, we can't provide absolutely everything. Everybody has different needs, different comforts that they leave at home when they come to work. Sometimes it's just too impractical. But it's always worth asking yourself as a leader, "Is that something we can reasonably incorporate into the workplace?"

> Part of treating people right is having the openness and flexibility to allow them to pursue their passions and use their skills—even if it's not in the job you initially hired them for.

Humans usually change and realize things about themselves over time: new interests, a passion they didn't know they had, a skill that can be put to use. Part of treating people right is having the openness and flexibility to allow them to pursue their passions and use their skills—even if it's not in the job you initially hired them for.

Because we've created such a strong community, there is an implied permission for individuals to ask for what they need. This community has also made it quite a bit easier and less threatening to bring a new or innovative idea to the table. The competitive advantage of a successful community is that it allows you to make full use of the collective IQ."

On their own, most individuals are capable of innovation, creative and critical thinking, and, most importantly, problem-solving. They are at their best with these skills in their own tribes or communities, like at home with their family or with their closest friends. With a strong sense of community at the office, an increased comfort level to share those personal skills takes on a life of its own.

In addition, my observation has been that many workplace cultures have not been sufficiently crafted, whereby the individuals involved can express or share their personal skills and assets in terms of outcomes for the *group* rather than just the individual. It is obvious to see that business culture in general is more about "look what *I've* done" rather than "look what *we've* done." Even the practice of evaluating employee performance is skewed almost completely to the individual rather than the team. In this environment, what would you expect the long-term outcome to produce?

My experience has shown that it creates the *opposite* of a healthy community. Individually focused companies often find employees isolate their ideas and creativity, try to problem solve on their own, and not share nearly as much creative and critical thinking.

If we are able to create, grow, and sustain a healthy community in the workplace, then the focus will shift from transaction to relationships—both business and personal—as well as customers.

This paradigm shift is likely the most important concept of all, as we will see.

CHAPTER 14

Relationships Are More Important than Transactions

Over time, I came to see reaching out to people as a way to make a difference in people's lives as well as a way to explore and learn and enrich my own; it became the conscious construction of my life's path.

—KEITH FERRAZZI

When I worked at the Chicago Board of Trade, most of my interactions were simply transactions. They weren't deeply meaningful relationships. I came in, did my job, got my paycheck (sometimes—ah, the life of a trader!), and went home. I had little interest in having a meaningful relationship with people on the trading floor. I'll admit that some of this attitude was by choice, but a great deal of it was simply the environment itself.

Because I had spent so much time in a transaction-oriented environment, I equated transactions with success—and success with money. The default driver was always, "I have to do the transactions. I have to sell." Unfortunately, I think many sales professions—particularly the financial services profession—have far too many people who are focused on the transaction solely.

I know because I was one.

For the most part, I am not saying that this is unscrupulous behavior, but I am saying that many folks are missing the opportunity to add significant satisfaction from the softer side of what we do as a profession. I mean, we are around new people all the time! Why would we not approach the opportunity to create more value in a new relationship than we would in a simple sale? For me, the hunt to close the transaction and make a dollar for its own sake lost its luster once I became aware of something that was much more important: relationships. And I found a way that I could do business with people that was much more fulfilling.

You have to be intentional about making your life relationship driven rather than transaction driven. To do that, you have to slow down, listen to, and appreciate what other people say. Tony Hsieh, the founder of Zappos, writes about this in his book, *Delivering Happiness*. If you've ever bought anything at Zappos, you'll know that the customer service is remarkable. If you have a problem or a question, you call the service line, and the people you talk to are just amazing. Tony Hsieh's leadership is one of the main reasons for this.

The previous standard metric for customer service calls was how many calls you could handle in an hour. Hsieh changed the paradigm. He asked instead, "How long can you make each call last?" He wanted each customer service representative to take fewer calls so that they could make each call longer.

The result was that the folks in the call center started to develop personal relationships with the clients—to the point where when some customers would call in, they would request to speak to a specific representative, because they had a connection with that person. It meant that people were looking for a reason to call Zappos. It meant that people wanted to order more stuff from Zappos. I have to imagine that this shift made the work much more meaningful to the call center staff as well. They were no longer disconnected pieces of a big machine; they were human beings responsible for creating relationships with other human beings.

The shift to slowing down and working on personal relation-ships is a big part of Hsieh's philosophy. It's important to note that if this philosophy exists, then the workplace permissions must also exist that allow the employee to execute what is asked. If you actually slow down and take the time to develop relationships, it's likely going to make employees happier, because it will make their jobs more fulfilling and make them care more. It's also going to make clients happier, because it will make their interactions more fulfilling, and they will be able to tell that employees care about them. This, in turn, will make them want to continue doing business with your company—no matter what business you are in!

For the most part, I can't think of many clients of Lakeside's that I'm not at least casual friends with. Some I'm closer with than others, but I can't think of any clients with whom I have a purely transactional relationship. They don't seem like business relation-ships to me, antiseptic relationships that only involve checking off the boxes and getting them out of the meeting. We usually spend easily half of any meeting talking about other stuff—what's going on in their lives, how their kids are, what they did over the weekend.

And then a relationship develops where we really care about each other, until there's virtually no line between the friendship and the business relationship.

I've even told clients, "Even though we're friends and this is *your* money, I expect that if I'm not doing what you need me to do with it, that you would feel guilt free about going somewhere else to get what you need. I would not hold that against our friendship."

I do think the interaction can get muddled if you are not able to separate business and friendship when appropriate. You could let your friendship cloud your judgment when it comes to what needs to be done on the business end, so we are constantly monitoring our process to ensure the quality of the work.

Interestingly, developing a deeper relationship with clients actually helps me be an even better advisor. Money is one of the most intimate things in your life. It is extremely personal, and as much as we might wish it didn't, a lot of what we do in our lives centers around money. Most everything we do is affected by it in some way. So it's very helpful to know as many deep, personal, and intimate things about my clients as they are willing to share in order to give them the best possible advice. The truth is, I'm as much a psychiatrist as I am a financial advisor!

By focusing on the relationship, even the moments when I have to give bad news can be a positive experience. Behavioral finance guru Nick Murray talks about financial advisors' tendency to want to avoid conflict. Because of this, we can shy away from calling our clients when the markets do poorly, for example. However, calling a client when investments do poorly and emotions are riding high actually gives me the opportunity to delve into their fears and find their pain, to really understand what is going on. Consequently, I've taken a situation where I was really nervous about their reaction and turned it into a conversation that actually deepened our relationship.

Having real and meaningful relationships with clients and with coworkers always makes the process more enjoyable—no matter what process you are engaged in. It feels better to be able to think of my interactions with associates as relationships rather than transactions. For me, a relationship-centered life is more fulfilling and enjoyable. And the truth is, if you focus on relationships, most of the time business aspects will take care of themselves.

If clients believe that I care about them, then I don't have to worry about asking them for their business. Treat people right, and they'll want to do business with you. Create a relationship with them, and they'll want to do business with you even more—just like Zappos. If you build a relationship with the people at your neighborhood furniture store, you're a lot more likely to buy your furniture there, even if it would be cheaper to buy it online. You'll go out of your way to visit your favorite coffee shop if you've developed a rapport with the baristas there. When the people who work in those stores develop a relationship with you, rather than just treating the interaction as a transaction, it makes you want to go back.

A client who has a positive experience is much more likely to be loyal. If I can't communicate to a client that I care about him or her as a person, rather than just caring about their business, there's a pretty high probability that the relationship will be transient. The bond is less meaningful, easier to break.

The same is true for employees and colleagues. If you care about the people you work with, your workplace becomes a lot less replaceable. If your coworkers are like your family, then if you replace your job, you're replacing your family members too—and most people don't want to do that. If you like the people you are working with, you are much more likely to stick around and even work harder for each other!

This concept is something we take into account early in the hiring process. When we are hiring somebody, at least on the higher level, we have the candidate come in and talk to the relevant stakeholders. We would generally include at least some of the people from the department in which the candidate would work in. If we're hiring on an executive level, each of the company's partners then take turns meeting with the candidate individually for lunch or dinner.

Why? Because we want to evaluate not only the person's skill set; we also want to make sure that we like him or her. This may seem obvious, but if we're going to spend 160 hours a month with this person, we should want to enjoy being in each other's company don't you think? I want to like and care about this person as a human being. That will ultimately make his or her work, and *my* work, better.

When you care about the people you work with, the workplace becomes more enjoyable, more fulfilling, more rewarding. When you're as excited about the people as you are about the work, it becomes a place that you *want to be* instead of a place you *have to go*.

* * *

The same excitement can also exist in the client relationship. However, in this day of quickly advancing technology and convenience, we must be careful that we don't dilute the experience by losing the opportunity to engage face to face.

Years ago, there was a commercial for an airline that showed an office full of salespeople. The business they're working for is slipping. The boss comes into the office and hands everybody a plane ticket from whatever airline it was. "Boss, what's this for?" the salespeople ask.

"For business," the boss replies. "Doing business on the phone and on email is good for a while, but every once in a while, you've got to add the personal touch."

Obviously, the purpose of this ad was to advertise the airline, but it also made the point that no matter how convenient technology might make things, there's no replacement for face-to-face interaction. That's why I've found that in many cases, visiting a client's physical business location can be an incredibly good use of my time.

After their kids and their family, the thing people are most proud of is what they've built their business or career into. So when I have to meet a client out of the office, I always try to make extra time to stop into the businesses of other clients who work along my route—and I encourage all my advisors to do the same. I stop in and ask them to give me a tour of their space or tell me about a special project they are working on. There's nothing better than seeing the pride they take in their workplaces and knowing that this extra effort on your part is building a stronger relationship.

Building a relationship with someone means appreciating and caring about the things that they care about. Of course, we don't have the capacity to genuinely, deeply care about everyone—and that's okay. Not every business transaction you make is connection worthy. If I go to a random convenience store and buy something, I'm not necessarily going to make a connection. But if I go to the same convenience store every morning to get my paper, and I see the same person behind the counter every morning, then I may start to make a connection.

You have to be willing to take the step to move the interaction from a transaction into a relationship. You have to show that you genuinely care. You have to slow down and take the time to actually listen and lean into the relationship.

Years ago, Carlos Santana, the amazing guitarist, was playing a show in Chicago, and I wanted tickets badly—as well as really good seats! So even though it was six weeks out from the show, I decided to call the ticket agent who was promoting the show and see what I could get. It was a Sunday, so I wasn't really expecting anyone to pick up. But surprisingly, a gentleman answered the phone.

"I'm interested in the upcoming Santana show—and I'm happy to pay for premium seats," I said.

It turned out this guy was actually quite senior in the company and had just come in on Sunday to get some extra work done.

"Well, normally we don't give the seats that you're looking for to anybody other than season ticket holders," he explained. "So we won't really know until just before the concert if there are any available, but if something comes up, I'll call you."

A week went by, and I didn't hear anything. I emailed the guy just to check in. "No, nothing yet," came the response, pretty much right away. Another week passed. I sent another email. This time I didn't get a response—until I went into the office on Monday morning and saw that he had emailed me back at one thirty in the morning!

His email said that there still weren't any tickets, so I emailed him back and said, "Thanks for checking. By the way, what the *hell* are you doing up and answering emails at one thirty in the morning?"

That was all it took to get the ball rolling.

He emailed back and said, "Ha ha ha. I've got a brand new baby girl, only three weeks old."

I immediately responded, asking, "What's her name?"

At the time, I had younger daughters myself, so I completely related to his situation. We exchanged a few more emails about his new daughter and girls in general until finally signing off on the conversation.

The next day, I asked my assistant to buy a baby girl gift (a pink blanket) that I could send to my new friend. We made sure to have his daughter's name stitched onto the blanket so it would be more personal.

A couple days later, he got the blanket, and he immediately called me. He was so appreciative of the gesture, especially coming from somebody who has daughters himself and really knows what it's like. "By the way," he said, after expressing his appreciation, "I got you some tickets for Santana." The seats were right up front, in the first couple rows. "Also," my new friend continued, "would you like to meet him?"

I couldn't believe it. "Uh, yeah!" I said. On the night of the show, about an hour before while the opening band was on, we were taken backstage with a small group and led into the greenroom. In front of us was Carlos Santana, wearing his white fedora and enjoying a glass of wine before the show started!

Now, when I got my friend that baby blanket, I wasn't trying to bribe him for tickets. It was honestly because I have three daughters, and he had just had his first daughter, so I really felt a connection with him. We maintained that connection, staying in touch over the years, and eventually, I became a new season ticket holder!

When I meet somebody, I always make it my mission to try to help them in some way. Do them a favor, make an introduction, cook a meal for them, give them some advice—or maybe buy them a baby blanket! The important thing here is that before I ask them to do anything for me, I try to do something for them.

What's really critical is that you can't keep score. That's an important point Keith Ferrazzi emphasizes in his book *Never Eat Alone.* You can—and should—make it your mission to proactively give somebody a leg up, but you can't come back a year later and say, "Hey, remember when I did that favor for you?" It doesn't work like that.

You should always make more "deposits" than "withdrawals" in a relationship, as my wife always says. You can operate at a deficit for a while, depending on your relationship with that person. But eventually, that relationship is going to require some deposits. Every relationship does. Personally, I always prefer to have positive balances in all of my relationship bank accounts!

Here is an example of what I mean.

A local businessman of significant wealth and influence was on my prospect list—and probably on the list of every financial advisor in the area. I was fortunately introduced to him by a mutual friend at a party and, after chatting for a bit, told him I would reach out in the near future and try to schedule a breakfast meeting. He gave me his mobile number and told me to follow up the next week.

A few days later, I tried "Mr. Smith" at the number he gave me, and the phone was answered by his assistant, Martha.

"May I speak to Mr. Smith, please?" I asked. "He asked me to call him after we met last week about getting together for breakfast."

"I'm sorry, Mr. Smith is not available right now," Martha replied. "May I pass along a message?"

"Yes—please have him call me at this number," I said.

Not surprisingly, I did not get a call back.

Honestly, I don't think I really expected one because he was—like me—busy and meets new people all the time. In addition, his assistant had no impetus to move me to the front of the line because I had not created any value for *her* either.

I tried the same scenario a couple more times over the next several weeks with the same results.

In the weeks that followed, I happened to be at our local high school football game on Friday night with some friends. We were watching the game and talking about our weekend plans when one woman said, "We are going to Martha's birthday party on Saturday night."

I said, "Is that the same Martha who works as an assistant to Mr. Smith?"

"Yes, it is," my friend replied.

"Tell her I said 'Happy Birthday' when you see her—I have had a couple brief conversations with her over the phone recently."

"Well," my friend continued, "her actual birthday is Monday, but we are celebrating Saturday with the party."

Guess what I did on Monday? I found Mr. Smith's phone number and called it as I had weeks previously, and, as usual, Martha answered.

"Happy Birthday to you …" I sang—to her delight.

"I remembered you called a few times in the last few weeks and asked for Mr. Smith's availability," she said when I had finished the song. "Would you like me to check his calendar?"

"No, I just heard it was your birthday through some mutual friends and wanted to wish you well."

The very next day, Martha *called me* (on Mr. Smith's phone) and asked if I could find an agreeable date to have breakfast with Mr. Smith.

Over the next few months, Mr. Smith and I developed quite a friendship, which soon turned into a meaningful business relationship. In addition, he has been the source of many referrals and an amazing ambassador for our firm.

Even though every relationship doesn't lead to a business opportunity, the ones that do are often so much more fulfilling—and actually lead to higher-quality work. Transactions are easy to marginalize. If the relationship is based on transactions, then it becomes a commodity. And when things become commodities, businesses start competing on price.

The truth is, if you're focusing on creating the best value for other people, on being the best you can be, on reaching your true potential—then you don't have to worry about competition at all.

CHAPTER 15

There Is No Competition

As far as competition goes, if you reach your potential, there is no competition.

—MARK W. CHAMBERLAIN

Let me tell you an important story:[6]

Once upon a time, a certain company had one hundred employees. At that time, there was a severe recession hitting the economy, and the company's business dropped off the cliff—as it did for companies all across the country. The accountants told the CEO that a 10 percent cut in costs was needed for the company to have any chance to survive the crisis.

---

6   This is the retelling of a story I read in the book *Tribal Leadership: Leveraging Natural Groups to Build a Thriving Organization* by Dave Logan, John King, and Halee Fischer-Wright (New York: HarperBusiness, 2011).

The CEO talked to his executive team and then called a company-wide meeting.

"We need to cut expenses by 10 percent," the CEO told the employees. "Either we can let ten of you go, or we can all stand together and ride this out by all taking a 10 percent pay cut—including me."

The decision was unanimous: rather than dramatically change the lives of ten families forever, everyone at the company decided to stick together and take the pay cut as a team and figure out how to help support each other. The effect this decision had on the "tribe," which was the company's culture, was immense.

If instead they had decided to cut ten jobs, how many would live in fear of being the eleventh cut if things got worse? How would these ten families—people who were part of their tribe for years—survive? How would leadership in the company be perceived knowing that the elite were the most protected? Banding together eliminated these fears and more.

Once united, these one hundred people worked harder and were more productive than they had ever been. They shared a goal: carry themselves and the group through the business cycle. The company not only survived but thrived—and they lived happily ever after!

In adversity, it's better to feel like you're in it with somebody else rather than that everyone's just out for themselves. In *Tribal Leadership*, Dave Logan, John King, and Halee Fischer-Wright explain that there are five stages of culture. Stage 1 is saying, "Life sucks." Stage 2 is saying, "My life sucks." Stage 3 is saying, "I'm great." Stage 4 is saying, "We're great." And Stage 5 is saying, "Life is great."

Logan, King, and Fischer-Wright estimate that nearly half of all organizations in this country operate at Stage 3. That's the stage of competition and domination, when all people are looking out for themselves. The higher stages are where the organization becomes a team, a tribe, and greatness is about pulling everybody up together.

Everybody has strengths and weaknesses. Instead of being intimidated by each other's strengths and competing with each other to see who's strongest, we can learn to use each other's strengths to lift up the whole organization, the whole tribe. It goes back to the idea of collective IQ—by combining strengths and IQs, you end up with something that is greater than the sum of its parts.

This is an important part of our hiring process. With all other attributes being equally qualified for a certain position, we try to take the approach of, "If it's different from what/who we already have, it might be healthy for the organization to add a different perspective." Diversity of race, age, background, personality, and skills are things to run *toward* rather than *away from*. If you have a homogenous approach to hiring, you are quite possibly limiting the potential of the collective IQ and your company's ability to grow. It would be like having a baseball team with nine shortstops. You'd probably never win a game.

If you're surrounded by people exactly like you, then you're probably going to end up stuck more than you need to. If you need to get past a wall, and you have only tunnelers, then when you can't dig a tunnel, you're going to be stuck. Once in a while, you need someone who thinks about ladders to get over the wall and sometimes people who have dynamite to blast through it!

My partners and I couldn't be more different. We share similar beliefs and values, of course, but the way we approach people, situations, and risk (to name a few) are very different.

Diversity also gives you the flexibility to match up personalities— whether that's in teams, for management, or even for mentoring. This is true for clients as well. We want to make sure that the client and the advisor fit together. All of our clients are different. We may have a client who doesn't work well with me but works super well with someone else who is the opposite of me. If you match an engineer with an artist, sometimes those two personality types just don't communicate as effectively as they should. Ultimately, if the mismatch is too great, it could affect the quality of the outcome for the client.

Another key concept that we try to remind ourselves to focus on regarding competition is who or what we are really competing with. There is a subtle but important difference between competing *externally* with other businesses that are in your particular line of work and competing *internally* with yourself and colleagues to reach your respective potential.

Externally, some common competitive aspects can be price, market share, service offering, and myriad other cosmetic metrics. One danger of spending too much time and effort on these externally focused qualities is the trap we can fall in about how they are measured. Once we begin to compare ourselves or our company in a spreadsheet format ("Let's see—we do it for this much, and they do it for that much …"), our goal is diminished to being incrementally better than a rival versus being the best *us* possible. Being incrementally better becomes a rat race of constantly measuring and comparing with an extremely narrow focus. It inevitably leads to marginalizing and commoditizing what you do.

An important component of striving to reach one's potential (as a company or personally) is the feedback loop you give yourself or your employees. Emphasizing the positive and deemphasizing the negative help create inspiration, celebration, and peer support. We can simultaneously emphasize the positive about each other, our teams, or ourselves *and* make learning from our mistakes a part of that positive experience. We so rarely give people the chance to talk about their opportunities for improvement in a positive way, so it's important to intentionally create those spaces. It's equally important to openly celebrate our achievements in front of our tribe. Humility is an admirable trait, but sometimes you just need to blow your own horn!

We have a biweekly meeting with our advisors, and we always try to make time at the end of the meeting to say, "Hey, somebody tell us a success story." It could be anything—getting a new client, helping a client with a tough situation, or even overcoming a personal obstacle.

When I hear about something great that someone did, I can appreciate and celebrate that with them—and it usually inspires me to want to do something great too. Cheering for each other's successes and outstanding achievements makes us all feel inspired rather than in competition with each other.

Greatness is not a zero-sum game in which if you get better, I am somehow diminished. The greater you are, the greater I am, and the greater *we* are. If you are able to achieve a higher level than me, that's good for *us*. That's a hard place to get to mentally, and it takes hard work and trust to get there.

One additional benefit of this approach is that once we stop looking at another business (or individual) as competition, we can actually start to *learn* from them—and they from us!

When we're honestly trying to reach our full potential, then we have no reason or even *time* to compete with each other. If we can just stay focused internally on being the best we can be, then we lift up the whole community together rather than tear it down or limit it through competition.

Then, if you are able to reach this nirvana, something amazing happens: you realize your almost limitless power to do good in the world.

CHAPTER 16

We Underestimate Our Power to Do Good

Not all of us can do great things, but we
can do small things with great love.

—MOTHER TERESA

Years ago, when I was in high school, my girlfriend and I were friends with another couple who were a year older than us, Mary and Jim. We were in many of the same clubs and activities together, so the four of us hung out and became good friends. After we graduated, we married our respective partners, we had kids around the same time, and we went to the same church. We spent a lot of time together. But in your twenties, life happens, and we ended up moving away to Chicago, while they stayed and went on with their own lives.

During the years our families lived in different cities, we really lost track of each other, but sadly, I did hear through mutual friends that Mary recently developed a very aggressive type of multiple sclerosis. Still, it would be a few more years before we moved back to our hometown and eventually ran into each other.

About five years ago, I saw Mary and Jim at the grocery store. This encounter turned into one of the most important lessons I have ever learned about people.

On that day, I pulled into the parking lot and parked as usual. Once I started walking toward the entry doors, I noticed a woman sitting in a wheelchair outside the store, but I was still too far away to recognize who she was. I assumed that she had been dropped off there by someone to wait while they parked the car and came back to assist her. As I neared the entrance, I could tell that the woman in the chair was Mary. Inexplicably, at that moment, a horrible thought went through my head—a thought that I am ashamed to think about today but hope you will be able to learn from for tomorrow.

The voice in my head said, "I don't have time to stop and talk to anybody right now. I haven't seen her in years, plus she's in a wheelchair, and I wouldn't even know what to say anyway." (Classy reaction, eh?) As I entered the store to grab my cart and start shopping, I was still talking to myself.

"Why would I intentionally avoid someone like that? I am not in that much of a hurry, and I haven't seen her in years!" I vowed to myself right then that if I were ever given another chance by the universe, I would be a better person.

Well, as the universe often does, it gave me my second chance five minutes later. Mary came around the corner of the aisle where I was, with Jim pushing her wheelchair.

I quickly walked over, shook Jim's hand, and bent over to give Mary a hug. We chatted for several minutes about what was going on in our lives, work, kids, and a few other niceties. We shook hands and hugged again, and I went on my merry way. The whole encounter was less than ten minutes.

As I walked away, I thought, "That's more like it—you did the right thing! Thanks, Universe!"

The problem was, I still didn't know why it was the right thing. The universe was not done with me yet.

A few aisles later, the three of us crossed paths again and again exchanged a brief pleasantry. What happened next changed me. It allowed me to have a better understanding of the effect of how I interact with other people affects *them*.

"Hey, Mark." Mary said with a weak voice. "Thanks for taking the time to stop and talk—it meant a lot!"

Wow.

At that moment, I was reminded of the power that we all have— every one of us, in every moment, big or small—to do good. I had the ability to change Mary's day by doing nothing more than stopping and talking for seven or eight minutes. It didn't cost me anything, but it meant so much to her. And to think that, at first sight, I had just completely (and intentionally) ignored her and walked by.

When I tell this story, I get a lot of head nods. It doesn't make me feel any better about my behavior in the beginning of the story, but it tells me that a lot of people, if they are being honest with themselves, have had a similar experience. It also tells me that there's a lot more every one of us could and should be doing to create those little moments of goodness.

We all have that power within us to do incredibly kind acts— with little effort other than our awareness. We just need to slow down long enough to realize it's there. Every day, every one of us has an opportunity to have a moment like the one I had with Mary.

If you think through your day yesterday, there's probably a moment when you could have stopped and taken some small action, said a kind word or put forth an effort that wouldn't cost you anything but a few minutes of your time.

Doing good doesn't have to be some big, grand action. People get stuck thinking, "I don't really have enough money," or, "I don't really have enough time," or, "I don't have enough information to really make a difference." We get stuck in the mindset of, "Whatever I do, it's not going to make that big of an impact."

Doing good is just as meaningful if it is a small gesture. Those little things tell somebody you are making them more important in the moment than you are making yourself.

A great example of a small but influential act is the handwritten note. In my opinion, it's a lost art in today's technology-packed world. It's so much more efficient to type out an email or text and send it on its way compared to the time it takes to handwrite a note and find a stamp, an envelope, and a mailbox. But that's the point, isn't it? Kindness isn't always convenient.

I think we often dismiss or minimize our opportunities to spread kindness because we underestimate the power of a small and simple act. If you refer back to the title of this chapter and Mother Teresa's quote, you realize she came to the same understanding.

We think, "Well, I'm just one person going to volunteer on this one day. Will that really make any difference?" Yes, it will. Don't underestimate the effect it has to take just one day to volunteer—because a whole army of volunteers is made up of all the people who are just one person, taking just one day. The result is a great example of the butterfly effect.

Shortly after I'd read Keith Ferrazzi's book *Never Eat Alone*, I was starting to really make an effort to make some of these changes in my life. One of the first early experiences with my personal behavior modification experiment was on my drive to work in Chicago. I always took the Chicago Skyway from my home because it was faster, even though it involved a toll. For years, I took this same route, and since I always passed through the same toll booth complex, I eventually became familiar with many of the toll booth attendees—not necessarily by name, but I'd recognize them as I passed through.

One guy always seemed to be in a bad mood. He just looked miserable—like he didn't want to be there. Never had a smile. One morning, I noticed I was in his line, and I decided to take that little extra moment. When I pulled up, I made a point to be friendly and nice. "Hey, how are you doing?" I asked. He nodded but still didn't smile as he made my change.

"Listen," I continued. "I've been going through this tollbooth for nearly twenty years. And I want you to know that you are the best, most efficient attendant that I've ever had."

And for the first time in twenty years, I saw the guy crack a smile.

As I continued driving to work, I wondered if that gesture had made any difference. I wondered if this guy would go home tonight, and instead of being in a bad mood, maybe he'd take a moment of time on his way home to say something nice to somebody else or to do a small act of kindness and spread the goodness even further. I will really never know if any of that trickle down ever really happened, but that kindness certainly had a better chance to be paid forward because of my effort—which took all of six seconds!

Of course, I'm not infallible—not by a long shot. Despite my effort to be more aware, to do more good, I'm still a jerk sometimes. I still get frustrated. Please allow me to demonstrate by sharing a bit more embarrassing honesty.

The other day I was flying, and a woman with a cane was taking a long time to get on the plane. I'm not proud of it, but I was getting incredibly frustrated that it was taking her so long to board. Even though it wasn't her fault that she needed the walking aid and was taking more time, I was annoyed with her. I didn't say anything (thankfully), but I stood there internally shaking my head, being a selfish jerk.

The plane took off, and for the next three and a half hours, I sat in my seat listening to music and spent much of that time thinking about my behavior. By the time we landed in Chicago, my frustration had dissipated. The plane landed, and I saw this woman struggling again as she tried to get out of her seat. As a frequent flier, I knew that you could lift the outer armrest of the seat by pushing in the button underneath it. This made it much easier for her to swing her legs around and use her cane to stand.

"Oh, thank you!" the woman said. "That makes it a lot easier."

She got up out of the seat, and I asked, "Which bag is yours?"

"The white one," she said.

"Okay," I said, "I've got it. You walk ahead and get off the plane, and I'll follow you out and give it to you in the terminal."

Obviously, this was a better outcome—for both of us. She got the help she needed, and I stopped being an ass!

What was going through my head that I would find it necessary to be impatient with a disabled person, someone who wasn't going to make me any later because the plane was going to leave on time anyway?

I think it was because I was going "too fast." Too fast, for me, is an ongoing internal battle that supports the notion that I need to get past what I am currently doing in order to get onto the next thing. Literally, it is a constant state of living in the future. I wasn't slowing down and looking at the potential power I had to do good *in the present moment*. It was only after the long flight and some reflection that I realized I had overlooked that power because I was too busy, in too much of a hurry. I also realized that I had to be deliberate about slowing down. I had to work at the habit of taking those small moments to do good. I can't just think, "I'm going to be nicer." I have to actively teach myself that habit.

In *Start With Why*, Simon Sinek writes about the chemical reaction that happens in your brain when you do good. When somebody does something nice for you, your body releases dopamine, which makes you feel good. But when you do good for someone else, your body releases even more dopamine, and you feel even better. Interestingly, one of the characteristics of dopamine is that it's extremely addictive. Once you get a "hit" of it from doing something good, you're going to want to do it again.

All of this translates into the workplace as well. We think about the good things we do at work in terms of our jobs, but we don't always think of them in terms of the human beings we're sitting next to.

There are a number of Good Samaritan actions that can happen in an office with the right culture, where the people are aware that the little things they do for each other are the same things that they'd do for a friend or their children. By doing so, you're creating an environment in the workplace that *feels* good because people are *doing* good. People naturally want to come to work in an environment that feels good.

The same goes for clients. Of course, you're helping the client by doing your job, but you can also do good for them in small ways, whether it's taking the extra time to compliment them, call them on their birthday, or to send them a handwritten note for no particular reason.

Awareness and attention are keys to making this type of shift happen and making it sustainable. The trouble is, we spend much of our life on autopilot in many of our daily activities and relationships. It's not that we don't care as much about things or people over time; it's just that many (like me) frequently get distracted with what's next.

Think about the feeling when you buy a new car. It's exciting every time you get in it for the first few months. You wash it every week, keep the interior clean, and enjoy that new car smell every time you drive it. But over time, you barely think about that car in the same way anymore. Now it's just a way to get to work.

We can experience a similar phenomenon in many other areas of our lives as well, including in personal relationships and with coworkers and even clients. Again, it's not necessarily that we care *less* about these people or things but that our minds are already busy looking for the next new thing.

Time lets us get comfortable with the new things that come into our lives—which is good—but it also diminishes our focus and attention. We can lose track of just how important and special these relationships are to us even though they may have a little rust on them.

As an example, I can't help but think about my commute to work in the city. For twenty years, I drove to downtown Chicago for work. There were days when I would get home and honestly have no idea how I got there. I'd set out from the office, and the next thing I knew, I'd be pulling into the driveway. "How the hell did that happen?" I'd think. "I don't remember paying any tolls or making any turns." It wasn't that I wasn't paying attention while I was driving; the drive was just so routine that I didn't really register it. I didn't look at the trees, the views of the lake, or the landscape I passed.

How do I break the pattern, break the routine, slow down, and really have a more heightened awareness of the world around me—old *and* new?

If, as leaders, we could create an environment that fosters peoples' awareness and attention to doing good, it could fuel changes that go far beyond the workplace. If people experience this environment and develop their behavior in the workplace, what behavior do they take into the client meeting? What behavior do they take home?

When I talk with other CEOs who are like minded, who also believe in our individual power to create goodness, there's a feeling that we can make a difference not just with our employees at work and our personal lives but in the world as a whole—a kindness movement! Your culture and those around you can become real agents of change in the world that go far beyond the walls of your office.

That's a big dream, but it would be really cool if we could, as leaders, be a part of making it come true.

CHAPTER 17

Our Legacy

Legacy is not leaving something for people.
It's leaving something in people.

—PETER STROPLE

During an exercise to create Lakeside's mission, vision, and values, I was asked to think back and ask myself how the community or the world would be different if our company didn't exist.

It's a difficult and profound question.

It's easy to answer in terms of our physical work or the advice that we give and the way we give it. It's easy to answer in terms of the dollars that we put back into the community and the jobs that we provide for local people.

It's *not* so easy to evaluate if the culture we have tried to create internally will have an effect on the community as a whole.

Have we been good stewards of the privilege that has allowed us to prosper in the same community in which we live? Have the cultural changes we have made been strong enough for other companies and communities around us to feel their effect? Is the world better because we're in it?

Think of your business as George Bailey in *It's a Wonderful Life*. If, like George Bailey, you could see what the world would be like if you or your company never existed, what would you see? Obviously, your clients wouldn't be getting your services, and your employees would be working somewhere else. But what would be the bigger effect? If we didn't change lives, somebody else would. Would they be changing these lives more effectively or positively than we are? Or would our absence create a void that wouldn't get filled unless we existed?

It's a hard but good moral question to ask yourself. If you can't answer in the affirmative, then you probably need to change what you are doing or how you are doing it. Can you say, "If we weren't here, yes, people would still be getting taken care of. Employees would still have places to work. But they're better off because we are here and because of the way we do things." Even if you can't make that statement definitively, it's something to strive for and a great standard to set for the rest of the business community.

Building the legacy for a company is similar to building a personal legacy, which we discuss with clients when considering philanthropy. Personal philanthropy is generally not a spontaneous act; it is rather a planned, thoughtful, and intentional act or series of acts. The same can be said for building the legacy of your company as you work with intention to create the culture that supports it.

For clients, money is just a small part of your legacy, I explain. It's really behavior, the way you treat people, your values. That is your true legacy.

Part of the legacy I have always wanted Lakeside to leave behind is to have been a model for other workplace cultures. I want the owner of any business, regardless of the industry, to be able to say, "I want those kinds of employees. I want that kind of workplace culture. I want that to be the way the community views us."

Of course, there is a certain amount of personal satisfaction when we get complimented on our role in the community, but mostly I feel proud that people are noticing our behavior, our culture. To be clear, it's not my behavior and culture (although it starts with willing leadership)—it's Lakeside's. People aren't saying, "Mark Chamberlain this or that." They say, "Lakeside this, and Lakeside that." For us, that's the beginning of a legacy worth leaving.

A legacy can't be about individuals in a company, because those people will eventually retire or move on. A legacy involves creating a culture that will endure, to the point where it doesn't matter who is there, because the cultural expectation is ingrained. You have to think of the company almost as an individual itself, as something that has a life of its own that merely reflects the values of the people who created it.

As the leader, it may be part of your job to create the legacy, but it must go beyond you. If Apple was only Steve Jobs, it would have collapsed when he died. But it didn't, because he created something that went beyond just himself and the individuals who worked there. He created the desire and vision to make products that would not only change the world but the behavior of the people in it.

You might not think that you could describe a company by its behavior—but in companies with successful cultures, you can. Companies can have behavior and a personality. For example, I've always thought that the people who work for Southwest Airlines are, almost across the board, exceptional. In 2010, Southwest bought AirTran Airways and integrated a large percentage of the latter's workforce. For the first year or two, you could spot the former AirTran people. Even though they wore Southwest uniforms, it was obvious that they weren't trained by Southwest and certainly did not reflect the culture that longtime Southwest employees exuded. Southwest had developed such a company character, such a distinctive way of training people, that somebody from the outside could identify a Southwest person regardless of uniform.

It isn't only big companies like Southwest that have a distinct character. There are several chains of gas stations and convenience stores in our community of northwest Indiana. One of these chains, Family Express, has a surprisingly intense hiring and training process. The resulting employee behavior is noticeably different, in a good way, than your usual convenience store experience. Leadership at this company has decided that an exceptional customer experience is the priority—and the result is a community of raving fans! They are less distracted by wanting to be the biggest and more intentional about wanting to be the best—the standard by which others compare themselves.

Every company has a reputation, good or bad. If the company has a good reputation, created by a superior culture, it's usually more fulfilling and meaningful for the people who work there. The tribe can take pride in what they stand for. Meanwhile, how would you feel on the other side of that? How would you feel if you worked for a company that had a bad reputation locally, nationally, or globally? (I'm sure you can name a few!) How would it feel to drive into work every day, to have people see you walk into the building and know the company you work for has not made the community a priority?

I've heard it said that a person's true character is how he or she acts when no one else is around. The same is true for companies. It's not just how you act in front of clients and customers. You could take a shortcut, and the client would never know—but within the company you would know. Whether you're okay with it or not says something about the collective character of the company and its leadership.

If your company doesn't have a reputation, a character, then it probably doesn't inspire. As a company, we get to decide whether we are just going to take up space in this building or add value to people beyond what we do as professionals. Is it just a place to work that pays a competitive wage and has good benefits? Or have you created something with a deeper value? The same question applies to clients: Do you provide a good service or something more? We felt so strongly about inspiring this philosophy that we created a company tagline and hashtag to describe it: #makingmoreoflife.

The hardest thing about accomplishing anything enduring is that it requires patience and time. The challenge becomes balancing patience and time and still being able to move at a competitive pace. In many cases, we want immediate gratification, but the stuff that's really worth getting usually takes time. The price many pay for impatience is settling for inferior values and culture.

Impatience can derail the pathway to leaving a legacy. It's like building trust. It's not something that can happen as quickly as we might like it to happen. Establishing a company's place in the community—especially in our business—is about building trust. Things could be going well for five years when the economy is going smoothly, but how are you going to hold up during a stress test like a recession?

Thinking about *today* only is a version of me-first thinking. Thinking about the future—the effect your actions will have not just on you but on the world that you are leaving your children and grandchildren, is part of caring for others—which by definition is "others first" thinking.

The desire for immediate gratification also contributes to complacency by tempting us to rest on our laurels. It makes us say, "We're doing well, we're getting compliments on our efforts. This is great. I don't need to put in the work anymore. I don't need to work to make anything better, because clearly it's already good."

To be sure, it's okay to enjoy what you've done. It's good to take the time to celebrate success. It's the nourishment we need to continue to want to get better, and that can create a very healthy loop. I make another little improvement, and then I get to feel good about that for a bit, which encourages me to want to do it again. The complacency loop is not so healthy. You need to make sure that your success fuels further growth and improvement rather than an excuse to stop. It's dangerous to get complacent about your progress and your success.

In sports, when you win a big game, there's nothing like it. You take the night to celebrate. For the winners, they are right back at it the very next day, right back on the court trying to get that next win, that next championship, trying to create a dynasty. Great athletes never stop striving, never stop trying to do even better, to continue their success, to make it endure. This concept is as true for individuals as it is for organizations.

Another example of leaving a legacy is in understanding the power and influence our businesses have to do good in the world. Fortunately, it seems like there's a big movement to encourage that. As I have said before, I personally believe it needs to start with caring internally, making sure that your own house is in order. If you haven't instilled those values within your company, you certainly won't be able to bring them out into the world.

I believe it's part of a leader's responsibility, and part of a company's responsibility, to create an environment that fosters good, not just in the workplace but out in the world we interact with.

A great example of this concept can be illustrated in the world of philanthropy. We have always had a strong company culture of giving back of our time, talents, and treasures. I am proud to say that, as a company, we are as dedicated to our community as we are to our own success. But honestly, I'm very concerned about the next generation of philanthropists. This is where we as businesses in our communities can leverage our ability to do good.

We are involved in a lot of charitable organizations, and I have observed that when you ask the same groups of people for donations over and over, you start to experience donor fatigue, both from a financial and an inspirational standpoint. As board members, we keep asking, "How are we going to raise more money next year?" The answer is *not* "the same way we raised it last year." If you keep communicating in the same way you did thirty years ago, your results are going to diminish year after year.

What does the demographic composition of many of our charitable boards look like today? Are they reflective of our population as a whole? Today, there are more millennials than baby boomers, but most charitable boards do not reflect this.

I really could talk for another chapter about this specific topic, but my point is that we have *earned* the right to be critical about things that we are willing to roll up our sleeves and get involved in. This is part of the leadership role, part of our responsibility, and an example of our potential power to change the world.

To make it easier for our people to live by the same values that we as leaders consider important, it's vital that as a company, we demonstrate the significance of those values. Make sure your people understand they have more value than just what they do between nine and five o'clock. If they care about something in the community and want to help with it, that's a part of them, and we want to support that.

In fact, watching someone else lead by example is the way I was initially inspired to get more deeply involved in philanthropy and my community. The reason I first gave to charity when I moved my business back to Chesterton, Indiana, was because I was reading the local paper, and I saw a picture of a business leader I knew fairly well. He was standing in a pile of ashes, helping to dig out an unfortunate family that lost everything in a house fire. Beside my friend were several of the employees who worked with him—digging in on a Sunday morning *simply because it needed to be done.*

"Man, that's inspiring," I thought. "I would like to be able to do that someday." Immediately, I had a very different perception of my friend and the company that he led.

To be honest, I am not completely comfortable with my picture being taken or having my name in the paper. But if I don't do that, then I potentially miss the chance to inspire somebody else who might be reading the paper, like I was twenty years ago. If you're lucky enough to be a leader, there is responsibility that comes with it. We also must be aware of the opportunity that it creates.

In his book *The Coaching Habit*, Michael Bungay Stanier writes that the job of a leader is to create space for learning moments. I think the job of being a role model or a mentor can be expanded to a whole company. If I see our mission as a company as creating spaces for learning moments for the rest of our community here in northwest Indiana, it can inspire other people and companies. And if there are enough leaders who believe in doing good both inside and outside the office, it can create a butterfly effect. That is when real change can start to occur throughout the world—and that is a legacy worth leaving.

CHAPTER 18

Putting Down the Old to Pick Up the New

Life is a series of almost imperceptible moments.

—MARK W. CHAMBERLAIN

There's a famous hunting technique that has been used for years in Africa and parts of Asia by hunters and researchers trying to capture wild monkeys. It is commonly known in this part of the world as the "Monkey Trap"—and here is how it works:

Hunters take an object like a gourd and drill a hole in it just large enough for the monkey's hand to fit through. Then they add sand or pebbles inside the gourd to make it heavier to carry. The final step is to insert a lure into the gourd, such as a piece of fresh fruit, that will attract the monkey's interest. Now, when the monkey inserts its hand and grabs the fruit in its fist, the hole is too small to get its hand out. You would think that the simple solution would be for the monkey to drop the fruit, release its fist, and slide the hand back out—but it does not. The monkey views this sweet treat as too valuable to discard—which ends up being its undoing! Now weighted down with the pebble-filled gourd, the monkey becomes a much easier target for hunters to snare.

This phenomenon is a great metaphor for business as well as life in general. Our reluctance to let go of something we are hanging onto can have a multitude of consequences. As discussed in several chapters of this book, the willingness—and sometimes even courage—to let go and try new things can change our businesses and our relationships in meaningful ways.

In business, the "way we have always done it" mentality can become a huge roadblock for some companies in terms of culture, efficiency, and attracting the best talent. For example, as we discussed earlier, our company's search for the best possible talent required a shift in thinking about the hiring process. The discussion of benefits, for example, when talking to a prospective millennial hire, must take into consideration the demand for nontraditional and flexible options.

When I went through my massive shift in thinking in 2006–2007, I realized that making changes required two things. It required me to realize that there was another way of doing things, and it required me to stop doing what I was doing before. If I held on to my old way of doing things, I would remain trapped, just like the monkey.

Transformational thinking requires that you put something down to pick up something new. You must leave behind a transaction-based life to live a relationship-based life. You must abandon a me-first attitude to adopt an attitude that puts other people first. You must stop treating your employees like children to start treating them like adults.

Put down asking formulaic questions and accepting superficial responses and pick up digging deeper and having more meaningful conversations. Put down a dictatorial management style and pick up the practice of empowering, enabling, and engaging your people. Put down a focus on competition, and pick up a focus on reaching your personal and group potential.

One of the most damaging examples of hanging on to old ideas is the concept of preconceived prejudices—drawing a conclusion about someone's value or ability based on race, religion, politics, job title, sex, physical appearance, age, and so on. We know from behavioral studies that our minds are quick to draw conclusions about a stranger in the first few seconds as a basic anthropological means of preservation. Unfortunately, today's social narrative has helped take a simple survival instinct and turn it into a prejudgment of character and worth.

It's time for you to abandon your preconceived notions of who and what people are based on their job title, physical appearance, social status, or age. Leave behind some of those filters that are limiting to us and to others and embrace a discipline that says, "Before I decide who this person is and what she stands for, I'm going to get to know her. I may not like what I find out, or I might like it immensely. But I'm going to give her the benefit of the doubt. I'm not going to prejudge her."

It's human nature to dislike losing things. For the longest time, my mindset was that if I changed the way I thought, I would lose something. What a paradox it is for us to be able to realize that if we give something up, we can gain so much more!

It would be easy to say, "Why would I change anything? Business is good. Why would I risk our success by considering transformational change? It's just too risky." I can see the logic in that. Risk is frightening. Changing something you've done your entire working life, that you've relied on for the past twenty or thirty years, and starting something new can be incredibly scary and hard.

How do you overcome that fear?

A series of almost imperceptible moments.

One of the biggest reasons we don't change the way we do things is because it feels too big. It feels overwhelming and insurmountable. But changing your culture, changing the energy of your workplace, isn't really an event. Rather than looking at it as a big change, think of it as a series of small changes and small steps.

The word *transformation* makes many people think of some big shift that happens overnight, some huge watershed moment when everything changes. But that's not actually what usually occurs. Transformational change isn't an event. It's a process, a series of little victories. You'll most likely have some failures along the way as well, and you can't let those bother you or distract you. You must overcome your fear of failure. And you have to enjoy those victories and let them build on each other.

I once heard a motivational speaker talk about baby steps. When you make a resolution to start exercising, he said, you don't go out and immediately run a marathon. You don't even go out and run every day. "Don't make that commitment," he said. "Instead, make a commitment to put on your shoes and walk to the corner. Whatever else happens, happens. Perhaps when you walk down to the corner with your shoes on, you'll think, 'I might as well walk around the block.' Perhaps the next week, you'll think, 'Maybe I'll jog for a little bit.' But don't think about that. Just make the commitment to put your shoes on and walk to the corner."

Even if a small task feels insurmountable, you can always break it down further, into smaller and smaller steps, until you can take that first baby step. Jenn, our corporate communications manager, set a goal for 2018: to delegate setting up events to Kristen, our receptionist, so that Jenn could focus more on other tasks.

The first couple of times they tried the new arrangement, it failed miserably. Kristen is very busy, and when the event wasn't set up by a certain time, Jenn would start to panic and wonder if this change was even a good idea. Should she just go and set up the event herself? Because this was something Jenn had always had control and ownership over, it was hard for her to relinquish it so she could pick up other responsibilities.

It was uncomfortable—but eventually, Jenn realized that with change comes being uncomfortable. She also realized that instead of letting go of event setup all at once, she could start this transformation with baby steps. She and Kristen could work together for a little while. She could have Kristen start out just setting up the glassware or the projection screen. Bit by bit, she could pass over the reins to Kristen. This would help Jenn feel confident that Kirsten knew exactly what she was doing—and it would empower Kristen to know she could do it and that she had Jenn's confidence. Moreover, by working together, Jenn could learn Kristen's ideas and perspective and then have the benefit of their collective IQ, rather than Kristen just being an extension of Jenn.

Of course, breaking things down into small steps takes time. It means slowing down, and we all live at such a high velocity that it can be difficult to do so. We think, "I'm too busy to take all those small steps." But you must be willing to slow down because you *will* fail at some point, and that takes time as well. Understanding and embracing the time frame of change culture is a huge part of whether you will succeed. The biggest hurdle for most people is the time. We want to change, and we want it to be effective now. We don't want to wait.

Baby steps are what will make a lasting effect. It's how you build the solid foundation of transformational change. It's a marathon versus a sprint. If you start out going as fast as you can, you'll never make it to the end of the marathon.

The idea of taking baby steps (or, as we recently started calling them, "1 percent changes") is simple. But that doesn't mean running a marathon is easy. There's a subtle but very distinct difference between simple and easy. The ideas we've been talking about in this book are simple, but that doesn't mean they are easy to enact. It takes hard work. It takes flexibility. It takes a change in mindset—sometimes a whole paradigm shift. It takes getting over fear. It takes sometimes moving one step up and two steps back. And you must be ready to deal with that.

Making simple a reality is the hard part that takes a vision, determination, and a willingness to work hard. And frankly, that's why these ideas sometimes don't come into being.

Nothing we've talked about in this book is magic. It takes time, patience, and hard work. Transformational thinking is like a sea change. It doesn't just mean doing something different; it means a massive overhaul—1 percent at a time.

What's more, transformational change isn't a one and done deal. You must keep working on it, constantly. Hire consultants to come in once a year and take your company's temperature, just like you would get a routine physical at the doctor. Good leaders can help establish the culture of a company, but if they don't see this as ongoing work, it will evaporate—quickly.

A lot of this work is front loaded. It takes a lot of effort in the beginning to establish a new culture and a moderate amount of maintenance to ensure its survival. But if you do it right, you'll create multiple leaders within the organization who can help maintain this culture—or, ideally, an entire tribe of leaders who can truly embody transformational change on a grand scale.

You Always Have a Choice

In 1976, my dad took me on one of his business trips to New York. We were staying in a hotel across from Central Park. One night, as we were walking from the hotel to a restaurant for dinner, we passed a guy sitting on a bench in the park. Next to him was a coffee can with some change in it. He wasn't really panhandling, per se, but it was obvious he was in need of help.

As we approached the bench, but still at some distance, I noticed the couple ahead of us had dropped a few coins in the coffee can and then exchanged some brief words. As we got closer, I saw my dad examine this guy a bit closer. Then he reached in his pocket, pulled out a couple bills, and dropped them in the can.

I was stunned.

Not because it was a nice thing to do, but because I had never seen him give money to a guy on the street before. He just didn't do it, and I had no idea why this time should be different—yet.

"Thank you," the guy said when the money hit the can.

"You're welcome," my dad said.

The guy responded, "I will make good use of it."

When we got about twenty feet down the sidewalk, I looked at my dad and said, "I've never seen you give a panhandler money before. Why did you give *that* guy money?"

"Son," said my dad, "turn around and take a close look at him."

I turned and looked at the panhandler. "What do you mean?" I asked.

"Look at his hair, his fingernails, and his shoes."

I did as he said and noticed that the panhandler's fingernails were clean, his hair was as neat as he could make it, and his shoes were old and beaten up, but they were clean.

"There's no excuse," my dad said, "regardless of what your lot in life is, for dirty hair, dirty nails, and unclean shoes. You always have a choice. You always have your self-respect."

What I learned in that moment is that you are in charge of your own destiny. You can create what you want to create. If your desire is to be more engaged with your clients, you can do that. If your desire is to create an engaging company culture, you can do that. You get to send a different and transformative message to clients as well as your work colleagues. You are in charge of your own culture. You get to set the tone.

Believe me, you are already setting the tone.

What message are you sending?

"Well," you're probably saying, "this all sounds good, Mark. But how do I do this at my company? How does this work in my personal life? How do I use this book?"

Take a baby step. Find a small, easy thing—not always a simple process—but an easy place you can effect change: something you can measure, that you can notice. Start there. If you can choose to do that one small, easy thing, that act will be your first step in getting to the next change.

Transformational change comes through a series of almost imperceptible steps. The goal of this book is to show you how to take the first step. Perhaps you give an employee a little more freedom to do something her own way. Perhaps you take an extra five minutes and talk to the receptionist on your way in, asking just one or two deeper questions instead of the usual, "How was your weekend?" Perhaps you really *listen* to people's answers.

You can choose from a thousand tiny, easy steps that will start you on the journey to transformational change. You just have to opt to take one, and then the next, and then the next. It will take a while. And you will probably have ups and downs, trials and errors, along the way. I certainly did. I didn't come in, start a company, and say, "Okay, this is the way we're going to do things now." It has been a process of trial and error for sixteen years. And that process is far from over, so I have to continue to be willingly flexible and change as I make new observations and learn new things.

Transformational change never has an end. It is forever ongoing. Thirty years from now, people will look at the way we do things today and question them—as they should. This is an ongoing journey, an ongoing conversation, and I want to invite *you* to be part of it. If you decide to start working toward transformational change, I want to hear more! Please share your thoughts and experiences— successes, challenges, lessons learned. In many ways, we're on this journey together. Be bold, be creative, be empowered, and inspire those around you to do the same. If I inspire you to start making transformational changes, and you share your experiences with me, you're going to inspire me right back. We all win.

Now that you've finished this book, you have a choice. You can be passive, or you can be active. You can put it on the shelf and do nothing. Or you can make a change. I hope that you will join the movement toward transforming our workplaces, our lives, and ourselves—the movement toward making more of life!

EPILOGUE

The Hero School

To have more, we must become more—
the character must change.

—TIGER TODD

I imagine a fitting final thought would be to share a remarkable story that demonstrates how transformational leadership can truly change the world—even if it's 1 percent at a time!

I met an amazing man through my wife a few years ago. His name is Tiger Todd, and he was a successful entrepreneur who sold his business in the late '90s. Since selling his company, Tiger has enjoyed a second career in corporate consulting based on his years of experience in business. He also has devoted a large part of his life since the '90s to philanthropy—specifically the issue of homelessness.

Through his interaction with thousands of homeless people in his hometown of Las Vegas, Tiger was able to identify a pattern in their thinking, behaviors, and decision-making that changed his approach to helping them.

The results of his revolutionary approach speak for themselves. Since beginning his mission, he and his team of volunteers have helped nearly fifty thousand homeless people find their way off the streets. His process has evolved into the Hero School for the Homeless in Las Vegas, which I have personally witnessed in action as a volunteer in their programs. (If you'd like to learn about them and how you can contribute, visit www.heroschool.us.)

There are many more details I could share about this amazing program, but let's stick to the basic principle Tiger identified as the Four Habits of the Homeless—which, ironically, are almost the exact opposite of the four characteristics of the entrepreneur.

Because human brains evolve at different rates and under different circumstances, some leeway in behavior is understandable. However, Todd has observed quite consistently how and when these patterns emerge and what the strategy to retrain them involves.

HABIT 1: DEPENDENT THINKING OR BEGGING ...

... is the belief that asking for something of value before offering something of value in return is an acceptable way to interact with other people (e.g., standing on the corner asking for money). Retraining people to understand the concept of creating value by *earning* the right to ask for something by first performing a task or service is the goal of the Hero School. The service may be menial, but that's not important; what's important is that it instills the concept of a fair barter.

Conversely, a typical characteristic of an entrepreneur is **inde-**

pendent thinking: to first seek a method to create value in some way (time, talent, or treasure) that sets the stage for a fair trade.

HABIT 2: BLAMING ...

... is the act of portraying that all the negative forces that have encumbered a person's life situation have been beset upon them from *external* forces (e.g., "It's not my fault I was fired—I was treated unfairly."). Hero School encourages students to look inward at their decision-making process and assess honestly how *their* actions may be responsible for their outcomes. A secondary benefit of this assessment is to make them aware that they have more control over their own lives than they realize—that they have instead been giving away their autonomy!

Many entrepreneurs are skilled at taking the blame, even in some cases when it may not actually be their fault (e.g., "I stand for my team—the buck stops here.").

HABIT 3: LEARNING HORIZONTALLY ...

... is the concept of surrounding oneself with like-minded or similar social tribes. It is a form of confirmation bias. We have routinely seen groups of homeless people standing under a bridge comparing notes on their lives. They are teaching each other how to be excellent at being homeless while at the same time validating their position. A better solution is the concept of learning *vertically*. Instead of standing on the corner asking for money from a woman in a business suit, ask her how she became successful and for advice on how you could do the same. Surrounding yourself with people who can challenge you to achieve vastly improves your chances of doing so.

As an entrepreneur, I have had hundreds of conversations with more accomplished professionals, and that education process has been a large part of our success.

HABIT 4: TELLING YOUR STORY ...

... is a process whereby homeless groups gather and start telling you their life story: "I used to have a job and a wife, but then this happened or that," and so on. Typically, a story has a beginning, middle, and end. The problem created by telling your story while standing in front of your tent-home in the park is that your ending lands you *here*: homeless in the park. What Hero School tries to teach is to postpone your storytelling until the story can have the ending you really want. Part of your story, at some point, can be that you endured being homeless, and then you picked yourself up and changed your life—a much better ending!

The reason I share the mission of the Hero School and Tiger Todd is to raise awareness of the tremendous potential that leadership and culture in a company (any company!) can have on the rest of the world. Together we can cultivate a community of great leaders—and not just CEOs, but leaders at every level—who share the notion of doing well *and* doing good. If and when we reach critical mass on these values, we can then focus less on being successful and spend more time on being significant.

CPSIA information can be obtained
at www.ICGtesting.com
Printed in the USA
LVHW081007080920
665333LV00009B/93/J